HOW TO SU
AT PART-TIM

C000270174

HOW TO
Succeed at
Part-time Study

FRED ORR

Sydney
UNWIN PAPERBACKS
Wellington   London   Boston

First published in 1988
Second impression 1988
Unwin Paperbacks
Allen & Unwin Australia Pty Ltd
An Unwin Hyman company
8 Napier Street, North Sydney, NSW 2060 Australia

Allen & Unwin New Zealand Ltd
60 Cambridge Terrace, Wellington, New Zealand

Unwin Hyman Limited
15–17 Broadwick Street, London W1V 1FP

Allen & Unwin Inc.
8 Winchester Place, Winchester, Mass 01890, USA

National Library of Australia
Cataloguing-in-Publication entry:

Orr, Fred.
    How to succeed at part-time study.

    ISBN 0 04 305007 7.

    1. Students, Part-time—Time management.
    2. Study, Method of.   3. Students, Part-time—
    Life skills guides.   I. Title.

371.3′028′12

Set in 10/11pt English Times, Linotron 202
Printed in Australia by The Book Printer, Maryborough, Victoria

Contents

Acknowledgements

Writing this book on part-time study has been an intense part-time effort. Just like the students described in this book, I have dashed from home to work and back again, carrying computer disks all of the time with the hope of finding the occasional free hour or so to write. Frantic, frenzied and more than frequently frazzled—that was the picture during the researching and writing periods.

I would like to thank all of those people who helped directly and indirectly in making the writing of this book possible. Particular thanks are due to my wife, Rachel, to whom this book is dedicated. She offered comforting and consolation when the ideas were lagging. My children, Matthew, Vanessa and Katharine also helped by tip-toeing over the floor area directly above my home study—I should have had it more adequately sound-proofed!

Many colleagues have helped with constructive commentary at various stages of the writing. I would particularly like to thank John Clanchy at Australian National University and Stuart Millard, Pamela Twining and Betty Carter at the Sydney Technical College for their perceptive and lucid critiques of the draft manuscript.

Special thanks are due to the many clients over the past years who have shared with me anxieties and occasionally ecstacies about their study and work situations. The names of the clients described in the case studies have been changed to protect the confidentiality of our counselling sessions.

Finally, many thanks to Jill Hickson and her associates and to Patrick Gallagher and staff at Allen & Unwin for their helpful suggestions and advice during all phases of this project.

Preface

As a part-time student, you face a particularly difficult lifestyle: worker, student and social being (family member, relationship partner). To effectively squeeze the responsibilities of the roles of worker and student into the typical workday is hard enough. To accommodate relationship and home responsibilities as well becomes most difficult indeed.

This book is like a shoe horn—it helps you to squeeze the varied roles and responsibilities of the part-time student into the available twenty four hours of each day. With some diligent application and practice of the skills described in the book, you should be able to hobble through your days initially (new habits are like new shoes—uncomfortable at first). Later, there is every reason to believe you can blaze ahead and beat the clock by fulfilling your goals at your workplace, in the classroom and at home.

Before launching straight into the critical study skills for successful part-time study, it might be helpful to address the topic: Who are the part-time students to whom this book is addressed? To many post-secondary and tertiary education staff, they constitute the waves of grey flannel business-dressed students who flood onto campuses between 5 and 6pm, some quickly munching a take-away dinner, before commencing their evening lectures. However, studies have shown that young (or not so young) business people are but one segment of the part-time population. Other important groups of part-time students include mature age individuals, apprentices in the trades, people tending the home, and correspondence students. You will quickly note that these catagories are not mutually exclusive.

Why study part-time? You may well ask. Many students elect part-time study because they cannot afford to attend on a full-time basis. Others report that they were already involved in a career stream which could not be interrupted for full-time study. Some younger students said they preferred the part-time option because they would get valuable job experience concurrently. Most apprentices had no option; attendance at technical college was an obligatory part of their apprenticeship conditions. Some students were at home looking after the family and enrolled in part-time studies to put variety and intellectual stimulation into their days and nights. Individuals well advanced in their careers but lacking a formal academic qualification were studying to boost them over a promotional barrier or to qualify them to change their career. Some students travelling frequently or living in remote areas found part-time correspondence study to be the only option in gaining further qualifications.

What problems do part-time students confront? Many, many, many. Time is the persistent enemy of most part-time students and much of this book will deal with ways to get on top of the time factor. However, other problems often pose difficulties for part-time students. Little, if any, social life can be a problem as it can place stress upon one's close relationships. There is also that law which Murphy established: Work pressures or health problems increase proportionally and synchronously with the part-time study load. I would be remiss in not mentioning the very basic issue of persistence. A six or eight year long program of study looks like an eternity to most students. Many fall by the way simply because the routine stretches their patience and diligence to the breaking point. There are many more problems, but to list them might cast a very grey, if not black, shadow across this book and you, the reader. Let's look at the brighter side ...

How can this book help you, the part-time student? For starters, the book will address the time squeeze—how to get all or most of your daily tasks accomplished at work, on campus and in your home. No matter what type of course you are pursuing, you will share one common characteristic with other part-time students: having too much to do and simply not enough time to do it in. The time squeeze causes anxiety in most and panic in many. These undesirable feelings can be avoided by increasing your effectiveness in the basic skills discussed in this book: how to organise your days and manage your time more effectively; by applying efficient study skills (reading, notetaking, researching, essay writing, and taking exams); and by managing well your physical health and your emotional relationships.

This book is a very readable and practical guide to part-time study. Time and personal efficiency will be continuing themes linking the chapters. Case studies of working students will assist you in identifying strategies which you might apply. In certain chapters, practical exercises are suggested to help you develop more efficient and effective approaches to your studies and work.

You may well wonder what qualifies me to write this book. I have been a part-time student, have taught part-time students and presently counsel part-time students. I know the demands, the dilemmas and even the possible dementia which can result from part-time study. I have published a book on examination study strategies (*How to Pass Exams*, Allen & Unwin, 1984) and a book on work (*How To Succeed at Work*, Allen & Unwin, 1987). The present book on part-time study is a logical sequel.

How to succeed at part-time study is a practical and clear guide which will help you to succeed in your studies. Without further ado, let's get started. In order to make the most efficient use of your time (which will be a constant battle), turn to the contents page and select the chapters which have immediate relevance and importance to you. Get started on them and return to the other chapters when time permits or when the need arises.

Good luck in your studies and enjoy the book!

Fred Orr
Sydney, 1987

This book is dedicated to
RACHEL

1
Time management strategies

- *Minimising wasted time*
- *Sources of wasted time*
    Television
    Telephone
    Waiting time
    Commuting time
    Uninvited visitors
- *Saying No!*
- *Planning your time*
- *Long term planning*
- *Planning next week*
- *Daily planning*

Time is the daily challenge for most busy people, and part-time students in particular. You have but 24 hours in each day to achieve your goals at work and study. You also have your personal life to manage, not to mention time for sleeping and eating. Given the demanding schedule for most part-time students, it would be very nice to stretch the day to get more time. However, even with contemporary technology, we can not bend, bow, or break the time barrier. To be a successful part-time student, you therefore must become efficient and effective and use each 24 hours to maximum advantage.

Jennifer and Mary, two very busy people, were studying languages at university and running their own catering business. As business people in a most competitive industry and as single mothers, they faced very challenging days of non-stop activity. At work, many hours were spent meeting clients, discussing catering arrangements, doing billing, filing and correspondence, and preparing specialty foods for the catered parties and functions. Before and after work, they managed their children and homes. They then squeezed into these hectic days their classes, language laboratory sessions and their individual studies when and where they could.

Sounds like a frantic life, doesn't it? It certainly was. However, both Jennifer and Mary finished their degrees with honours and Mary progressed to post-graduate studies. How did they manage to survive in business, thrive at home and still excel at university?

Fundamentally, by being very good managers of time. We'll look at some of their time management strategies in more detail later in this chapter, but for the present, the important message is: If they can do it, so can you. The first step towards a more efficient and satisfying life style is to read this chapter and then *practise* the principles of time management. It's hard work and will probably require you to alter your daily habits, but the end result is well worth the trouble. There's no question about the difficulty in changing deeply entrenched habits, but the outcome will fully justify your efforts. Rather than focus upon difficulties, take positive action and press ahead right now and read this chapter.

This chapter will focus upon time management and efficient studying. The following practical strategies will be described to help you get more value from your hours, days and weeks. Firstly, minimise your wasted time. Secondly, maximise your study time. Thirdly, plan your tasks and budget your time—you will be surprised at how much more can be done following a few minutes of planning. Finally, make the most of small bits of time at home, at work or while on-the-go between here and there. As a part-time student, you will be familiar with frantic days and pressing schedules, so perhaps the utility of these chapter goals should be readily apparent. Without further ado, let's get started.

Minimising wasted time

If you were asked to estimate the amount of time you waste each day, you might well have difficulty giving an accurate response. Several years ago, I asked 200 part-time students to keep a daily log of wasted time over a two week period. How much time do you think they wasted per day? An average of 64 minutes. That might sound trivial, but the astute mathematicians amongst you will readily calcuate the weekly total of 448 minutes or almost 7½ hours of time wastage per week. That is simply too much time to ignore, especially when you are pressed at work, pushed in your studies and perplexed as to how to fit in some leisure activities.

As a learning experience, why not assess your own time wastage? Keep a daily log of wasted time over the next two weeks. Simply carry a small pocket notebook and when you find yourself waiting, procrastinating, daydreaming, or aimlessly wandering or wondering, make a few notes as follows:

Wasted time log

When:
Where:
With whom:
Why?
Total time wasted:

With the exception of the notes on *Why*?, the other items are straight forward and should present little difficulty. However, *Why*? questions potentially well-entrenched habits. Why was I daydreaming for 18 minutes when I was supposed to be studying French? Why was I speaking to Chris for 37 minutes when I only called to check the economics assignment? Why did Tom monopolise me for 22 minutes when he popped his head into my office saying, 'Got a second for a quick question?' These questions will cause perhaps some startling awakenings to habitual behaviours which are truly draining your already drying reservoir of time. No matter how much discomfort the notetaking might cause, do your best and keep at it for two weeks. You will be surprised at the results.

Consider your notes each evening and look for trends in your behaviour which will help to reduce wasted time. You might be interested to know the sources of time wastage which were reported by others.

Sources of wasted time

There are some traditional chinks in the armour of even the most stalwart students, workers and time managers. Heading the list are television and telephone time. Closely following you will find waiting time, commuting time and time spent doing jobs for others to whom the harried student/worker should have initially said emphatically, No! Let's look at each of these time wastage areas in turn.

Television time

The definitive solution for the busy person dashing between work and study—get rid of the TV! If this is a radical and revolutionary tactic, especially if you live in a family setting where others enjoy TV, try the following.

- Plan your viewing by ticking shows on the weekly schedule and then stick to your pre-arranged viewing schedule.
- Stand up while watching TV; it's easier to move away when the program finishes. You might also do some stretching and bending exercises to keep fit while watching.
- If you do sit down for a lengthy show, do something else while watching. Page through magazines, sew, file, write to those neglected friends—don't just sit there and vegetate, unless you have decided that TV is mental and physical relaxation time.
- For poor disciplinarians, set the oven timer for the program's finish time and move away at the sound of the bell.
- Try moving the set to some inconvenient or uncomfortable setting where you are not likely to linger for long periods.
- If you have a video recorder, record programs which are programmed at difficult times and watch them when convenient.

Telephone time

- If you have a receptionist/secretary at work, have your phone calls screened and messages taken when you are busy.
- Plan a telephone time each day and make all of your calls then.
- Try to limit your calls to set time. Some modern push-button phones can be programmed to sound a tone at a pre-determined interval to remind you that time is flying by.
- Be fully prepared to tell long-winded people: 'I've got to go now'.

- Make brief notes before important or complicated phone calls to make sure you cover the major items and limit any unnecessary digressions.
- Ask frequent callers to ring at a time convenient to you.
- Use a taped answering machine if no one is available to take messages.
- Do not let the telephone interrupt you when you are working or studying intently. See your local telephone salesperson about new models which have Do Not Disturb or Tone Off functions.
- If you are audacious enough to hang up on a long-winded caller, do so when you are speaking and then keep the phone off the hook. The other caller will think no one could be so self-effacing as to hang up on themselves and will blame the telephone system for the fault.

Waiting time

- Carry study materials and revise when waiting. Small revision cards fastened together by string or clips are very handy for short bursts of learning
- Avoid along waits for appointments by ringing ahead to check for any anticipated delays.
- Consider using a portable cassette player to learn key concepts and ideas. Just making the cassettes will be a helpful learning exercise.
- Think about the environmental conditions (wind, rain, crowding) where you general wait and organise suitable revision materials—plastic covered books, packs of note cards connected by string, lecture notes bound in a substantial folder, cassette tapes and playback equipment.

Commuting time

- Study on trains, buses and cars. Use revision cards if the conditions are crowded.
- When driving, use a cassette player to revise the key concepts from previous lectures.

- Learn an idea at each red traffic light. Plan to learn ten or so key facts or concepts every time you travel.
- When walking, revise a set of important concepts every time you step up on the kerb of the next block.
- Keep a pen and note pad handy to jot down ideas.
- If you travel with classmates, discuss the ideas presented in the last lecture. Actively using information is the best way to enhance learning and retention.

You might already be applying some of these ideas. If so, well done! If not, try them and see how your efficiency improves. Having read the above suggestions, you may be interested to learn how Jennifer and Mary managed their harried schedules and succeeded at their work and studies.

As you can imagine, much of the time in a catering business is spent standing at a sink or stove preparing and cooking food. The hands are active, but the mind is perfectly available to think and learn. Jennifer and Mary used portable cassette machines to revise key terms and concepts. The cassettes were played while working in the kitchen and while doing housework and exercising. Waiting time was either productively used or strictly minimised and an answering machine took messages. Most phone calls were made in a set period during the evening. Above all, most time was saved by careful and systematic planning of each day.

You might say that planning is desirable and good, but what about unforeseen events, like people who interrupt my work? Yes, uninvited visitors either at home or at work can wreak havoc with diligent workers trying to follow well planned timetables. What can you do about these intruders? Here are some suggestions.

Uninivited visitors

- Keep your door closed if you don't want to be interrupted. If you don't have your own office, consider changing the position of your desk so that you are less accessible to people strolling by—face away from the doorway so they can't catch your eye.

- Use a Do Not Distrub sign, either placed on your door or displayed on your desk top.

- If possible, try to have someone intercept visitors and take messages for you.

- Either remove extra chairs from your immediate work station or place files on them so that unwanted visitors cannot quickly be seated. Once that happens, it can be difficult to get them to move on quickly without seeming abrupt or rude (which may be necessary with persistent invaders).

- If you hear the office gossip coming down the hallway and you fear your office is a possible invasion target, get up quickly and meet them in the hallway. Do not allow the person to enter your workspace. Standing discussions are far shorter than sit down meetings.

- For persistent interrupters, tell them firmly that you are busy and cannot talk presently. If you wish, arrange a set time to see them when you are free.

- If an unwanted visitor manages to get into your office, and Heaven forbid, finds a seat, then immediately stand and remain standing. Pace around your work station looking frequently at your watch and uttering: 'Yes ... well ...; In summary then, ...'; and other phrases which act to terminate discussions.

- For the most thick-hided and insensitive invaders, just tell them you are very busy and cannot spare any more time. If you feel obliged, tell them when it is convenient for them to see you in the future.

Jennifer and Mary were lucky in that they worked from their homes and the only persons frequenting their doorsteps on a regular basis were people delivering the milk and the mail. However, they did report difficulties early in their careers when they found themselves on various committees. While some of these activities were very worthwhile and provided service to others and some satisfaction to themselves, others were an absolute waste of time. They wished they had said No! at the very start and not become involved. Let's look at this very common problem and how you can protect your time and energy by saying No!

Saying No!

Part-time students are certainly not immune to requests for time, favours, or personal involvement in apparently worthwhile causes and committees. Requests for your time or attention might include: helping out a colleague at work; loaning your lecture notes to a classmate who always seems to be absent from classes; working late to help a colleague when you have a class; serving on committees; and attending yet another meeting.

Saying No! appears to be a simple task. After all, it's only one small word, but as you will probably agree, it is often very difficult to say. Saying No! can be especially irksome when face-to-face with a friend, colleague, boss, teacher, or some other beseeching person. Many say Yes when they want to say No! mainly because they think they might be disapproved of or disliked. Having said Yes, they often experience anger, resentment, despair or even depression for having been weak. Saying No! under appropriate circumstances is an important time saver. Chapter 2, which deals with personal management skills, will present in detail how you can develop a more assertive stand with people who intrude upon your work, study and time.

Planning your time

In order to cope with the tasks, trials and torments which confront most part-time students, you will need to become a proficient time and task planner. The pressure is certainly intense when you have three major responsibilities—studying, working and managing personal relationships. The best way to maximise your effectiveness in these roles is to plan your time: in the long term, over the next semester or several months; over a shorter period, such as the next week or two; and in the next 24 hours, a daily time plan.

Before looking in detail at each of these time plans, complete the following checklist to obtain a general indication of how you are coping with the following time pressures which commonly affect part-time students.

Time management checklist

( ) I am frequently unprepared for meetings or special events.

( ) My work gets done in a helter-skelter fashion.

( ) I have difficulty sorting the important jobs from the trivial.

( ) Indecision plagues my days.

( ) I am frequently late for appointments

( ) Many jobs get started, but few are carried through to completion.

( ) My workmates do not see me as a reliable person.

( ) I have been passed over when jobs with greater responsibility are being delegated.

( ) My desk top or work space looks like a disaster scene.

( ) I have trouble getting started.

( ) My academic assignments are often handed in late.

( ) Studying for exams is left to the last week or two.

( ) My results do not reflect my potential. I should be performing better.

Don't be discouraged if you have ticked many of the items. To be human is to be fallible. However, the wise person monitors and manages the fallibilities which have been problematic in the past. The way to success is to learn from your experiences.

In order to maximise your opportunities for success, focus upon the common theme running through the above checklist— organisation. Getting organised is what most of us intend to do tomorrow, but the unexpected always seems to side-track us. One helpful and basic way of achieving a more organised approach to work and study is to *plan*.

Long term planning

A friend who advanced through the corporate hierarchy of a large multinational firm to ultimately become the chief executive officer was fond of saying: Scan the horizon frequently to find your target, but always plan your next few steps. This saying highlights the importance of long-term goals and step-by-step planning. Having a long term goal can be a strong motivator as well as a most effective guide to mapping your path over the coming days and weeks.

For the part-time student, planning your time across the next semester and giving careful thought to your career plans can boost your motivation. Given the pressures of work and study, any boost will be appreciated. Some of the following planning suggestions might well boost your motivation and progress.

- Establish a career file and clip job and vocational articles which relate to you.
- Periodically leaf through the file and reassess your present position. Jobs and people change and you might want to make a move.
- Keep up to date with the job market in your area of work. Scan the employment ads at least once a month to monitor fluctuations in the field.
- Talk with people who are experienced in your career area.
- Consider a transfer if your organisation is large and you can get more direct career experience in another department.

Tom was a department head in a softgoods manufacturing company. At 27, he had been with his firm for six years and head of his department for eighteen months. He was working part-time on a bachelor of business degree to advance his corporate career. Apart from the normal worries and hassles of part-time students, Tom was concerned about the possibility of a merger or take-over. Previously these corporate capers had only been of academic interest, but when news of a takeover spread through the firm, he became very concerned. Within weeks, he was called into the managing director's office and told that the company had indeed been taken over by a larger firm and that some radical changes might occur in the staffing and structure of the company. The MD suggested that Tom might keep a vigilant eye out for other jobs.

Six weeks later Tom was retrenched. In spite of his forewarning, his retrenchment was a shock as Tom felt he was a model employee and the firm would be crazy to let him go. However, crazy things do happen, much to Tom's chagrin. Unfortunately, he was caught with no immediate employment options. Instead of directing his energy into a systematic job search campaign, Tom slumped into a depression, letting his studies go as well. He withdrew from his course, went on the dole and generally spiralled downwards. After seven months of therapy, with copious morale boosting, he finally worked his way out of the depression and started looking for another job.

The lesson to be learned from Tom's dilemma is to keep actively aware of what's happening in your career area, no matter how buoyant and positive your career prospects might presently appear. Monitor your long and medium-term career options. Keep in touch with colleagues in related firms, attend work-related meetings, and read career publications. And, keep an up-to-date file on career possibilities.

Just as a well-organised approach to long-term career planning is highly recommended, the same principle applies to your studies. The time dimension in this case is shorter, perhaps stretching over the next year or semester, but the benefits of planning are just as valuable.

One way to plot your path in a time effective and organised way through the next months is to chart your major commitments on a semester plan. You can see at a glance where the heavy periods are—the weeks where reports, essays, projects and assignments are due. Try plotting your commitments on a chart similar to the one on p. 13.

The chart shows the fourteen weeks of the academic semester numbered across the columns, and the subjects listed on the left in the rows. Within the various columns opposite the respective subjects are noted the assignments, tests and other commitments of the student.

Most part-time students will be doing one to four subjects in any one semester. In order to appraise your study and work commitments concurrently, you might want to note as well any major work tasks which are going to compete for study time. Remember, Murphy's Law states that work pressures will increase in

Semester-at-a-Glance Chart

	Weeks													
	1	2	3	4	5	6	7	8	9	10	11	12	13	14
A		- →												*Exam*
			- - - → Ass.			- - - - - - - → Ass.								
B		- - - → Rpt.		- - → Tst. - ↗ Rpt. - - - - - - - → Prj.									*Exam*
		- →												
C		- - - → Ess.			- - - - - - - - - → Ess.								*Exam*
D					- → Tst.		- - - - - - → Prj.						*Exam*
		- →												

Key: *Tst* = test   Ass = assignment
Rpt = report   Prj = project

direct proportion to your academic load. Having entered your academic commitments and the work-related tasks about which you are presently aware on the Semester-at-a-glance chart, you will be able to organise more effectively the next months and weeks.

There are several very important features to note in the chart. One, you will see that each major task has a lead-up arrow. The arrows signify the estimated preparation periods necessary for each task or project. There is absolutely no sense in trying to prepare a 5000 word essay or report in the early hours of the morning when the assignment is due. Even if you churn out the required number of words, the product probably will be of very questionable quality. Good writing requires good re-writing. The operational message here is to start the task several weeks prior to submission date and work steadily upon it, giving yourself adequate time for drafting and revising. Turn to chapter 6, Writing reports and essays, for a more detailed discussion on time and task planning for these major assignments.

A second feature to note in the Semester-at-a-glance chart is that the longest arrows extend from week two to week fourteen, terminating in the examination for each subject. The more casual student might respond with consternation and puzzlement. 'What!? Start studying for examinations in week two of the semester! You must be crazy!' These are perfectly normal and common reactions to the suggestion that exam revision should start very early. No one likes to even think about exams that early in the semester, let alone sit down to learn their notes. However, no matter how distasteful the suggestion might be, it does have clear merit. Regretfully, many students fail exams or perform far below their potential because they simply started revising too late. Don't tell your friends that you're staying in on a weekend morning to revise for your exams which do not begin for another thirteen weeks. They're certain to think that the stress of part-time studentship has affected you. However, smile secretly to yourself, retire to your studies and then smile proudly when you receive your final results.

In summary, organise your months and weeks by systematic long term planning. To fulfil your work and academic responsibilities: start early; work steadily *and* plan your long term goals.

Planning your next week

Most people work comfortably and effectively by keeping the next week in mind and planning their movements accordingly. This is particularly true for part-time students who have obligations and responsibilities arising at work and in their studies.

With your semester plan in front of you, you can see at a glance what projects need attention in the next week or two. Take special note of academic tasks which will earn you marks such as reports, essays and tests. Spend a few minutes on Monday morning and plan how you will arrange your time over the next two weeks to achieve optimal use from the time available. It is very likely that you will have to shuffle your priorities, especially if you have a major test scheduled a week from Tuesday.

When planning your time over the next two weeks, try to maximise your efficiency but do allow sufficient flexibility for the unexpected. When you tackle a complex set of responsibilities such as working, studying and sometimes relaxing, there is bound to be an occasional surprise or infrequent hiccough. You want to be adaptable and flexible so these unanticipated events do not jolt you into panic. You will quickly discover the positive feeling of meeting these surprises and crises with calm and deliberate action. Your colleagues who do not plan their time or prepare strategically for major events would probably panic if Auntie Nell from the country dropped in for high tea the afternoon before an evening exam. Planning assists preparation, which prompts peak performance.

Daily planning

The most important period of time to plan is *today*. After planning the semester and then the next two weeks, writing out another plan might well sound pedantic. However, the time and energy you save by planning your movements over the next 24 hours will quickly justify the small effort. Perhaps you have experienced some of the following situations because you did not plan your days.

- You arrive at work dressed inappropriately for a special event that day.
- The telephone bill somehow got lost in the shuffle and your phone has been cut off.
- You remember your mother's birthday 24 hours late. She told you it really didn't matter, but you know otherwise from the way she dabbed the tears from her eyes.
- Your phone call on Friday for weekend theatre tickets produced the response: Sold out two days ago.
- You fail to check the final timetable for the end of year exams and discover that your exam for today had been re-scheduled for yesterday.
- You double back on your trail to do things which should have been done before.
- You forget a medical specialist's appointment and receive an account for the full consultation fee.

- You attend a critical meeting at work but failed to prepare adequately. The boss asks you to comment upon the Jones project. You stammer and faulter.

Some of these situations are just plain irksome, but others might justifiably send shivers up your backbone, especially if you have violated the trust, reliance and responsibility engendered in you by others—notably your boss, relatives and personal friends. How can you avoid these embarrassments? Full marks if you respond: Daily planning!

Organising your days by writing a daily plan is more than just drawing up a list of tasks and chores. There are three important elements in an effective daily plan: (1) a precise description of the tasks to be done; (2) assigning priority rankings; and (3) an estimate of the time to be spent on the tasks. A fourth element which you might add after each job is done is a tick, written with gusto to reinforce the positive feeling of accomplishment. Let's look at a sample daily plan.

Daily plan

Tasks	Priority	Time	Done
Telephone:			
Jim-schedule meeting	1	2 mins	
Carol-retrieve lect. notes	3	5 mins	
Trupac P/L-contract ready?	1	10 mins	
Write:			
Outline Smith report	2	30 mins	
Letters:			
Greenbrier-quote	1	20 mins	
Council-query rates	3	10 mins	
Economics essay-revise	2	30 mins	
Meetings:			
Staff devel-10:00	1	45 mins	
See:			
Robert re squash	3	5 mins	
Mike-Darlington job	2	15 mins	
Buy:			
Razor blades	3	5 mins	

Tasks	Priority	Time	Done
Pick up:			
Dry cleaning	3	3 mins	
Deliver:			
Exercise:			
Tennis-8:30pm, Ken	1	75 mins	
Pay:			
Electricity bill	1	3 mins	
Renew NPA journal subscrptn	3	3 mins	
Miscellaneous:			
Winter holiday-skiing???			
Work out cost estimates	3	10 mins	

This is but one form which a daily plan might take. From the above example, you can see the types of entries you might consider including. Remember, the plan is a very individual document and should be adapted to your own individual needs and life style. Design it, experiment with it and change it so that you develop a system which works for you. Like all skills, the more you practise, the better you become at planning and living more efficiently.

Jennifer and Mary became experts at daily planning. Their shopping trips, food preparation chores, domestic duties and studies were all planned, generally the night before. The more relaxed and casual readers might think all of this planning sounds a bit excessive, but the busier you are, the more necessary planning becomes. The results speak for themselves. Ask any busy and successful person about planning and you will have these views validated.

Checklist

( ) I minimise wasted time by carrying study materials to read or revise while commuting and waiting.

( ) I always try to do something else while watching TV.
( ) I concentrate my telephone calls into one period when possible.
( ) I plan my telephone calls and set time limits when speaking with garrulous people.
( ) I say No! to myself and others when distractions prevail.
( ) I plan my days and tackle difficult jobs when conditions are optimum for task completion.
( ) I monitor developments relevant to my long-term career goals.

Summary

This chapter has presented a range of strategies for managing your busy schedule as a part-time student. The major points to note are:

- Minimise wasted time. Keep a record of wasted time and find ways to avoid these situations in the future.
- Be particularly careful about time spent watching television, speaking on the telephone, waiting for events to happen, commuting to work or class, and socialising with uninvited guests at your work station or study place.
- Spend time planning for the future and today. Long term, middle range and daily planning will pay bountiful dividends in the form of greater efficiency, less hassle, more leisure and higher productivity.

2
Personal management skills

- ● *Dealing with procrastination*
- ● *Asserting yourself*
- ● *Negotiation*
- ● *Delegating skills*

Winning the war against the clock will be a constant challenge for part-time students. As suggested in the preceding chapter, planning tasks and allocating time are very important starting points. However, planning, but then not *doing* will hardly win diplomas, gain promotion or enhance your self esteem.

Melanie worked as a field officer for a trade union and was slowly proceeding through a welfare certificate course at technical college. Her job was quite hectic—administrative and clerical chores at head office and field calls to factories where she liaised with shop stewards and counselled union members. While dashing through her work days from head office to field visits, she tried to squeeze in some study time, but her best intentions rarely were fulfilled.

Even though she was very bright and perfectly capable, she failed one subject and was given a supplementary examination in another. She approached the course coordinator and pleaded a case of increased job responsibility and diminished time for study, but her plea was ineffectual. The coordinator recognised her potential, but insisted that she must give more time to her studies. Melanie wrote detailed study plans, but she rarely implemented them. Studying was given second priority when others needed her attention.

We've all known what it's like to establish a work plan but then fail to do it. Putting your plans into action can be a major battle. There are always those papers to go through, phone calls to make and a myriad of other 'urgent' duties which keep us from getting started on the really important tasks. Procrastination is one of the most common sources of frustration both at work and when studying. We are all vulnerable to this ever common problem and much like a disease, we can suffer gravely from its effects.

This chapter will address several important personal management skills, focusing especially upon how to handle the common problem of procrastination. Crucial skills to be discussed include assertiveness, negotiation and delegation. Applying these skills should assist you to achieve more of your personal goals, experience greater satisfaction in your work and study, and boost your confidence. At the conclusion of this chapter, you should be ready to assert yourself, negotiate with your boss and teaching staff, and delegate tasks where appropriate. Let's look firstly at procrastination.

Procrastination

As suggested above, procrastination is putting off until later what should really be done now—or should have been done yesterday or earlier! The reasons why people put off certain jobs can be categorised conveniently under the following headings: dislike for the specific job; fear of failing to do the job correctly; and perfectionism (I'll wait until the job can be done *perfectly* before I start). Perhaps a short case study will help to illustrate the problem.

Peter had been working for three years as an assistant administrative officer in the federal taxation office and studying for a commerce degree part-time. He had completed about half of his degree but progress had been slow. Peter planned a career in management, but advancement and promotion were contingent upon completion of his course.

From the heading of this section, it will come as no surprise to learn that Peter's major stumbling block was procrastination. Peter, a very methodical and seemingly well-organised individual, could readily tell you his one, three and five-year goals, but when asked how progress was going, there would be a slight hesitation while Peter generated relevant and plausible excuses. Yes, he was a good planner, but a very weak implementer. He was far more proficient at making excuses than completing his work. However, his excuses were eventually discounted at work and at university. How did he break out of this difficult procrastination problem? Here are some of the pointers which he applied following our counselling sessions.

ANTI-PROCRASTINATION STRATEGY

- Get settled at your work place and clear away distractions.
- Make certain you have all necessary materials readily available to minimise interruptions.
- Write down the specific task you wish to accomplish first and the time you plan to finish it. Be realistic when planning your tasks and time allocations.
- Plan your tasks for small periods of time. Write down what you will accomplish in the next fifteen or thirty minutes, thus allowing little opportunity for task avoidance or daydreaming.
- Set a reward for completing the defined tasks. Small rewards can help to motivate you towards task completion.
- Challenge any temptation to put the task aside because you cannot complete it *perfectly*. Perfectionism can be a major menace. Far better to get started on the task and then reshape your efforts as you go along.
- Analyse fears of failure or other relevant emotional reactions which are hindering your start or progress.
- Convert 'Can I ...?' questions to 'I can!' exclamations after realistically appraising the task.
- Try to establish a positive habit of getting down to your tasks at a specific time. Time will then become a stimulus for the start of productive work.
- Divide large jobs into manageable tasks.
- Tell a work colleague what you expect to accomplish in your next work period. Your progress report to your colleague will act both as an incentive and hopefully as a reward.
- Expect to succeed. Imagine yourself accomplishing your set goals and then get into action.
- Avoid 'what if ...?' type thinking. Worrying is counter productive and it can be minimised with practice.
- Read chapter three of *How To Succeed At Work* by F. E. Orr (Allen & Unwin) which addresses the procrastination problem in more detail.

Peter planned each day but he found it necessary to ask himself, What is the *most important* job to get working on right now? By considering his priorities and then acting directly upon his decisions, he was able to avoid the temptation to spend most of his time on relatively trivial tasks. He also posted a slogan in front of his desk: *Time is opportunity!* While he was able to beat the procrastination problem most of the time, the campaign had to be maintained continually. With a steady assault on the problem, generally he was able to make the most of each day and to maximise his opportunities.

Beating worries

Worrying is a most time-consuming activity which prevents many people from getting on with their high priority jobs. Try the following suggestions about dealing with worries.

- Confront: face the worry, don't avoid it.
- Talk: discuss the problem with a friend or counsellor.
- Plan: approach the problem in steps.
- Relax: reduce the tension by relaxation.
- Laugh: see the humorous side.
- Think: look at the problem from diverse perspectives.
- Exercise: work the tensions out with exercise.
- Be positive: identify and maximise the positive side.
- Assert: read the next section.

Assertion

How often have you said to yourself: I won't make waves right now; or, I'll deal with this person/problem another day. Most people tend to put off confrontations, especially if the matter involves a prickly person or a peppery problem.

Before going further, it might be helpful to define assertiveness. Operationally, assertiveness can be defined as the responsible expression of one's feelings and thoughts to the particular person(s) at an appropriate time. It differs from aggression in that your communication should be responsible and sensitive to the situation and feelings of the other person(s). In order to become skilled in asserting oneself with one's classmates, bosses, teaching staff and family members, planning and practice will be necessary.

Let's consider an example. Susan worked as a childcare assistant in a large kindergarten and rushed off to classes three evenings each week for lectures in her child welfare certificate course. The only complication in an otherwise very full and satisfying work/study schedule was Marjorie, a colleague of Susan's. Marjorie, according to Susan, was a user. She often asked Susan to help with extra duties and then took all of the credit for the joint venture. Marjorie was doing the same certificate course, but skipped classes regularly and would then beseech Susan for the class notes. Susan was initially sympathetic but the crunch came when Marjorie had not completed a major assignment and wanted to use Susan's completed paper to 'just get the basic ideas'.

Susan was getting angry at being consistently used and abused by Marjorie. This last request was just too much to tolerate. She sought counselling to discuss her anger and how to deal with Marjorie. Susan initially feared saying No! to others, especially to colleagues at work. However, after practising some assertion exercises, Susan happily reported that she had said No! most assertively and effectively to Marjorie. Susan was also surprised to find that Marjorie actually started to respect her for her new strength of character. The working relationship changed from subservience to civility. Susan blossomed while Marjorie moved her attentions elsewhere to less assertive and more compliant classmates.

Susan's dilemma is surprisingly common. We have all walked away from difficult interpersonal situations saying, 'It's not worth making a fuss'. But if you have felt angry within yourself for not having said what you wanted to say, then perhaps you could benefit from assertiveness training.

Part-time students are particularly vulnerable to requests for time and favours as many are still in training positions. Such requests might include helping out a colleague at work; loaning your lecture notes to a classmate who is frequently absent from classes; acquiescing to your boss' request to work late when you also have an evening class; serving on committees; or being given duties which more senior employees choose to avoid. All of these activities can drain your already impoverished supply of time and energy—and make you very angry as well.

Saying No! appears to be a simple task. After all, it's only one small word, but as you will probably agree, it is often very difficult to say. Saying No! can be especially difficult when face-to-face with a friend, colleague, boss or teacher. Many say Yes when they want to say No! After saying Yes, they often feel angry for being weak.

There is no sense buying into anger, resentment and remorse when these negative emotional states can be avoided. Practise saying No! It might help if you stand in front of your bathroom mirror and repeat that critical word over and over, perhaps even using some strong inflection to emphasise your feelings. In addition to these rehearsal sessions, you might also try the following.

Becoming more assertive

- Anticipate when you are likely to be asked for favours or for your time. If you want to say No! then rehearse beforehand. When the time comes, do it!

- Write out short scripts custom-made for particular people who have wrangled time and favours from you in the past. Read the relevant script prior to your next meeting with the problem person(s).

- Consider your non-verbal behaviour: eye contact, gestures, posture, and facial expression. What you do with your body is just as important as your verbal message. Once again, practise in front of a mirror to see yourself as the other person will see you.

- Keep your message short and concise. After delivering your message, depart from the scene with dignity and aplomb. Avoid protracted discussions as they can erode the effectiveness of your message.

- Read Fensterheim and Baer's book, *Don't Say Yes When You Want To Say No* (Futura Books), an excellent and practical book on becoming more assertive.

- If you experience continuing difficulties with assertion situations, then consult a psychologist who is experienced in assertiveness training. Saying No! emphatically is a skill which can certainly be learned and developed.

In essence, managing these difficult interpersonal situations will require you to be a skilled communicator. Plan your approach, practise thoroughly and then put the plan into direct action. Some of your early assertion attempts may well fail, but you should persist. Every time you try, you will learn, regardless of whether the situation ended positively or negatively. Reflect upon your experiences and maximise the strong points and minimise the weak ones.

Negotiation

Negotiation skills might seem to be an unusual topic for part-time students, unless of course you are studying labour relations. For those outside the industrial relations field, being a good negotiator is a critical skill, especially when time is short and conditions for work and study are marginal.

Tom joined the state railways as an apprentice electrician and was attending technical college one day per week. He was progressing well with his work and part-time studies until his third year. At that time, he was given more work responsibilities, thus diminishing the already small amount of time he had for studying. Tom was keen to move ahead and fulfil his new responsibilities, but he simply needed more time for his studies. He mentioned the problem to his immediate supervisor who was unsympathetic. Undeterred, Tom made a tactful approach to the section boss requesting some additional paid study leave. The request was granted, but only after some firm bargaining. Tom ultimately finished his course, having learned almost as much about negotiating and the practical politics of organisations as he did about his electrical trade.

Many part-time students will experience a similar plight to Tom's—being pressed for study time after accepting further job responsibilities. Should this scenario confront you, follow the steps below when making a submission to your boss for more study time, preferably on full pay. The same procedures might be adapted to negotiate extensions on major assignments from your teaching staff. Rules applying to these matters might be considered general guidelines. It's up to the individual to present a strong case with full documentation (supporting letters, certificates) when the relevant rule needs to be adjusted.

Plan your case

Be prepared to ask for additional time, opportunities or improved conditions. You have every right to ask, but when you do ask, be certain that you present a strong and well prepared case. Imagine a situation at work when you wish to request additional time off work to prepare for the yearly exams. Initially, jot down ideas about your request. Be certain to consider how your course of study will enhance the job you are presently doing. You might want to note particular headings from the course curriculum which have relevance to your work. When you have collected your thoughts, and perhaps the thoughts of some colleagues to get a well-rounded perspective, then try scripting your actual approach. The script is not meant to be delivered word for word, but it is valuable preparation in sorting out the issues clearly and concisely. The following guidelines will be helpful.

- Identify yourself and your position at work, if the person you are speaking with does not know you.
- Specify why you are there: 'I would like to discuss the possibility of additional study leave prior to my final exams'.
- Point out specifically any positive aspects of your work and study to the organisation.
- Nominate the exact number of study hours needed and the relevant dates.
- Regardless of the answer or outcome, thank your boss for the opportunity to discuss the matter.
- Leave positively—head up, eye contact, firm handshake, if appropriate.

Rehearse

Having planned your case, it is now important to rehearse your performance. Much like an actor preparing for a stage play, work out a script and then read it perhaps five or more times so that the main points are retained. Stand up and imagine yourself at the place where you will speak with your boss; preferably a private place where you can speak in confidence.

You might well find it helpful to rehearse your case at home in front of your bathroom mirror so that you can see how you appear. A further refinement in the rehearsal process is to tape-record your delivery and then replay and listen critically for points which need improvement. The final test is to have a close friend whose judgment you respect play the role of your boss as you deliver your case. Ask for criticism so that your approach is as positive, persuasive and effective as possible.

Perform

The day will come when you have scheduled your interview and it is perfectly predictable that you will be somewhat nervous. In fact, you may well be *very* nervous, even to the point of losing considerable sleep the night before. Don't let that worry you, for if you have been sleeping well in the long term, one night's restlessness will not hinder your performance. Go easy on the coffee and tea in the hours preceding your interview, as you will probably be keyed up enough and your system will not need additional stimulation. Think positively and fortify your courage by repeating a short slogan, such as 'I can do it!'

Appeal

There is always the possibility that your approach may be unsuccessful. Should that be the case, most bureaucratic systems have appeal procedures. In small businesses, your case will be directed to your boss, so consider the opposing arguments, looking for any relevant points to justify your appeal.

In a case for additional study time, you might want to broach the possibility of making up the additional leave during the summer recess period when there are no classes. In most negotiations, there are generally some grounds for further discussion. Prior to putting forth an appeal, it would be very helpful to discuss your case with an experienced negotiator, perhaps a union representative, so that you have a comprehensive picture of the possibilities.

In Tom's case, he was well prepared and sensitive to his boss' thoughts and opinions about leave policy and he was able to successfully negotiate extended study time. He did, however, have to make up the time during the summer recess. Interestingly, when he completed his apprenticeship, he entered the political arena where his negotiation and assertiveness skills were certainly put to the test!

In summary, negotiating for various concessions such as more study time, assignment extensions and other work–study issues will require you to become a very skilled communicator. Know your opposition, prepare thoroughly, practise arduously and then perform impeccably. Tall orders, yes, but certainly achievable with practice.

Delegation

One way through the time traps of work and study is to find others who are willing to help. You are familiar with the expression: Many hands make light work. If your work load or home duties are too heavy, then lighten them by recruiting others. There's absolutely no reason why you should not appropriately share your load if others are benefiting in some way from your work.

Julie was a single mother living in a communal house with two other women who also had children. Three adults and five children living in the same house made life hectic and harrowing at times, but generally everyone seemed to get along very well. Julie was attending university to prepare for a career as an editor in the publishing industry. She worked four half-days a week as a secretary in a publishing firm and did some freelance typing to earn extra money. Juggling duties and time between being a mother, worker and housemate filled the days very quickly, but she still had to find time for her studies.

The solution to Julie's time problem was delegation of some

duties. In order to assess her situation, she composed a grid with columns for Work and Home at the top and Duties and People down the left side. She filled in the four boxes to find possible paths through her very busy days.

From the grid entries, Julie saw several possibilities for delegating duties at home and some potential sources of extra efficiency at the office. She constructed shopping, cooking and cleaning rosters and delegated (following a group conference) the children and adults at home to these duties on two week intervals. The office situation was more delicate, but Julie was able to argue a strong case for employing a casual office assistant to take over the photocopying and other routine office duties.

These delegations provided several additional hours per week, allowing Julie to progress considerably with her studies. She is almost finished with her degree and is presently looking forward to working full-time as an editor. The diplomacy and tact which allowed her to delegate many duties will certainly be strong assets in handling the sometimes fragile egos and pernickety personalities in the publishing trade.

Delegation skills

- Assess your work and home situations critically, looking for opportunities to share the workloads.
- Consider the personalities of the people whom you might approach. What are their sensitivities and how might you best broach the topic to them?
- Be fair and show how you can contribute to the efficiency of the home or office.
- If you strike an impasse, do not desert the plan. Reconsider and discuss a new plan with the individuals.
- Lateral thinking can be an advantage. Discuss your ideas with an open-minded colleague or friend to extend your thinking.
- Above all, be diplomatic and tactful in your dealings with your colleagues, family and friends. Antagonising these individuals will only create more problems.

In essence, delegating duties requires some inventive thinking and diplomatic dealings. The personal communication skills you develop in establishing more efficient work and home schedules will be strong assets when you leave your part-time studies and enter the full-time work force.

Checklist

( ) I get to the important jobs and consciously avoid any temptation to procrastinate.

( ) I work through any worries—I don't allow them to work through me.

( ) I assert myself appropriately at work and at study.

( ) I negotiate when circumstances warrant.

( ) I am aware of appeal procedures and use them when appropriate.

( ) I look for opportunities to delegate duties and responsibilities fairly.

Summary

This chapter has described personal management skills which can assist the part-time student in progressing more efficiently and effectively both at work and and at home.

- Combat procrastination
  —Get settled at your work/study place with all materials at hand.
  —Write a specific plan for each session.
  —Finish each job—don't leave with it half done.
  —Break large jobs into manageable tasks.
  —Do not allow worries to infiltrate every working hour.
- Become more assertive
  —Think carefully through the whole problem.
  —Plan what you are going to say and how you will do it.
  —Practise your delivery several times before the crucial day.
  —Following 'the performance', consider how you can impove for the next time.

- Negotiate for better work/study conditions
  —Think ahead.
  —Be tactful and sensitive to the feelings of others.
  —When unsuccessful initially, prepare an appeal.
- Delegate duties when possible at work and home
  —Be fair.
  —Help others and they will be more willing to help you.

These skills can be learned, but as they generally involve complex dealings with others, careful preparation and practice will be necessary. A final word: *try*! You will learn from your experiences, even the ones which are not so successful.

3
Listening and notetaking

MELDRUM

- *Hearing v. listening*
- *Pre-lecture activities*
- *Listening during lectures*
- *Practical pointers for active listening*
- *Notetaking*
- *Practical notetaking strategies*
- *Notetaking symbols*
- *Post-lecture learning activities*

Rick, a twenty-year-old marketing trainee for a national chain of department stores, was faltering in his part-time commerce studies. After finishing his work days at five pm, he dashed off to university to attend his 6–9 pm lectures three evenings a week. He was not performing well at all in his studies and feared that he might lose his traineeship if he did not improve.

One symptom of the malaise which affected Rick's studies was manifest in his lecture notes. They were a disaster and essentially indecipherable. On one page, there were a few words and phrases in the upper left hand corner and some meandering lines further down the page. I asked Rick what these meandering marks represented and he confirmed my suspicion: sleep.

Rick agreed that performing well in his assignments and exams was to a large extent contingent upon good lecture notes. Random pen marks on a note pad are simply not going to be helpful. We discussed various ways of improving his performance, starting with active listening and careful notetaking.

This chapter will describe practical pointers which can help you to get more value from your studies by becoming a more effective listener and notetaker. The difference between hearing and listening will be discussed followed by strategies which you can implement before, during and after lectures to ensure the best possible set of class notes.

Hearing *v.* listening

Many people believe that hearing *is* listening. How many times can you recall sitting in class apparently listening to the discussion when you were asked to comment upon the present point. Even though you thought your eyes were open and you seemed to be involved in the discussion, you did not have even the merest inkling about what had just gone on in the class. You did hear the discussion and the invitation for you to comment, but you were not *listening*. Embarrassing, yes; enlightening, no!

It can happen to all of us, but when you are wanting to progress with your studies, daydreaming and slumbering in class are most counterproductive.

So, what is the practical difference between hearing and listening? The situation above suggests that hearing is the reception of sound waves. Correct. Listening, however, involves much more. To be listening, your brain must actively process the sound waves received by your ears. The impulses are transmitted to the brain, interpreted and then stored in either short or long term memory. If you are taking notes, a series of muscle activating impulses must be sent from the brain to your writing arm and hand so that notes can be recorded on your notepad. Sounds complicated and a bit like hard work, doesn't it? The simple truth is, listening *is* hard work. However, don't let that put you off. You can develop your listening skills so that you listen more effectively and efficiently. Here are some steps which you should try to improve your listening skills.

Pre-lecture activities

The process of active listening should begin well before you enter the lecture hall or classroom. In order to attend actively, you should prepare yourself by doing some preliminary reading. What should I read? For starters, you should read the course syllabus so that you have a general idea of the course organisation and it is hoped, the goals of each lecture.

Most course coordinators will have a syllabus which should be available to the students. The syllabus may have recommended texts and suggested readings corresponding to each lecture. If all of this information is on the syllabus, you're in luck. If the suggested readings are omitted, then organise your own background reading or ask the lecturer for recommended sources.

Pre-reading

Pre-reading for lectures does not imply thorough and time-consuming study of every paragraph in the relevant chapters. On the contrary, it means a quick, perhaps five to ten minute overview of the chapter. As you are paging through the text, run your eyes down over the columns of print and take special notice of section headings, bold print, italics, pictures, graphs or any other visual aids. Some texts are what the computer people call 'user friendly'. That is, they have been designed so that all of these features almost jump off the page to impress the reader with the meaning of the material. However, other texts might be decidedly 'reader unfriendly' and you will have to work quite diligently at extracting the major themes from the text.

While you are going through the pages, jot down on paper the major ideas and concepts and note the titles of graphs and charts. It is perfectly fair to assume that features that are specially depicted or represented in the text are likely to receive special attention in the lecture. Experienced students will be familiar with the exasperating situation when a lecturer slaps a transparency onto an overhead projector and makes a few cursory comments about a complex chart or graph. Just as you have drawn the axes of the graph on your notepad, the transparency has been removed and the lecturer has progressed to the next point, leaving you feeling angry, frustrated and bewildered about the essence of the chart.

Pre-reading can help you considerably. You will know whether the chart is in your text. If it is, sit back and listen actively and attentively to get the major point, having noted the general topic in your notes. Leave notetaking about the chart until that evening when you can consult your text and get an accurate representation down in your notes. Your classmates on either side will probably be sweating and straining as you sit back listening actively to the lecture.

Having prepared for the lecture by pre-reading, you will be familiar with the terms and text and you will avoid all of the indecision about: 'Should I take this down or not?' The value of pre-reading has to be experienced. Try it prior to your next lecture. There will be no turning back once you know the benefits.

Review notes from previous lecture

One additional pre-lecture activity is very worthwhile. That is reviewing your notes from the previous lecture while you are waiting for the class to start. As most lectures will probably follow some logical or developmental path, a quick review of the notes from the previous lecture will help to warm up your mind to the present topics. That short review will also pay dividends at exam time, for every time you go through your notes, you will be strengthening your retention and facilitating your understanding of the concepts. So, don't just sit there wasting time. Use it to your advantage.

Listening during the lectures

Any novice teacher who is still learning the fine art of effective lecturing could probably recount a wide range of tales about student behaviour during lectures. Amongst the repertoire we might hear about students reading the daily paper; testing the aerodynamics of new paper airplane designs; discussing current affairs (both public and personal); and of course dozing, sleeping or Heaven forbid!, snoring. Disgraceful? No, not really. Attentive listening is hard work and students can become distracted if the lecture is not topical and interesting.

However, chatting, gossiping, reading, or even sleeping in the back rows will not win you high marks in the exams. Given that the tertiary education lecture tradition has persisted for hundreds of years, you might as well accept the necessity of becoming an active listener. The skills you learn will very likely be helpful to you in your job. Here are some pointers which should help.

Practical pointers for active listening

- Be certain to have functional pens and adequate notepaper so that you are not distracted by faulty or insufficient equipment.
- Concentrate on getting the central ideas and major concepts. Try to differentiate between key concepts and illustrative matter.
- If you are being distracted, change your seat, close the window, draw the shade or take any other necessary action so that you can concentrate on the lecture.

- Sit in the front of the lecture hall. Studies have shown that students who sit at or close to the front of lecture halls generally perform better academically than those who sit at the back.

- Maintain a flexible and adaptable listening style. Be prepared to tolerate the idiosyncrasies of the lecturer.

- Do not relax too much when the lecturer digresses with jokes or anecdotes. Rest your writing arm briefly and enjoy the interlude, but be prepared to get back into action when the lecturer returns to the central theme.

- Avoid boredom and mental stagnation by trying to anticipate what is coming next in the lecture.

- If hand fatigue is a persistent problem, some muscle training is advisable. Practise taking notes from TV programs, during meetings or during any other discussion to strengthen and condition your muscles.

- Speaking speed ranges between 120 and 180 words per minute, whereas we can think at four to five times that rate. It has been estimated that we spend about 27 minutes per wakeful hour listening. However, only about seven minutes is *effective* listening. Push yourself to boost that figure by thinking ahead, anticipating and evaluating.

- As a hedge against your eventual examinations, listen for good examination topics and make a marginal note opposite any point you believe to be a good examinable point.

In summary, taking good lecture notes requires very active listening. Approach your lectures as opportunities to test your concentration powers. Strive to leave each lecture with a set of notes which represents accurately the major points. You will become a more effective listener as you consistently press yourself to practise the skills noted in this section. Listening is hard work, but your academic record and your performance in your job will certainly improve as you sharpen your listening skills.

Notetaking

Notetaking seems to be an expected function of most students involved in upper secondary and tertiary studies. However, classes or basic instruction in notetaking skills are rare, as teaching staff often assume student proficiency in this skill once students have reached upper secondary or tertiary levels.

Molly, an ex-stenographer and shorthand typist, is an outstanding exception. She had spent sixteen years as a most efficient secretary, but decided to attend university to broaden her career horizons. She assumed that the best way to handle the notetaking situation was to take down every utterance of the lecturer and then transcribe her shorthand notes. Yes, she was most adept at taking notes, but unfortunately she carried her skills to excess.

Two days prior to her final examinations, Molly came in to see me with a very heavy brief case and red, swollen eyes. She had been crying, but not from the strain of carrying her heavy case. She realised too late that those fully transcribed and neatly typed notes which filled her case were simply not going to be learned before the exams. All of her time had been spent preparing those exhaustive notes and there was no time left for learning. Her approach might have been appropriate for court room stenography, but not for the university lecture hall. She certainly should have been selective in what she chose to record—and not included the lecturer's anecdotes, jokes, and sundry digressions from the major theme. Molly failed her exams, but she was allowed to return to try again. She was a much wiser person in her second attempt.

Most students will have limited experience in lecture notetaking prior to tertiary studies. Therefore, this section will set out some basic guidelines which you may wish to practise. It is important to point out that notetaking is a very individualistic skill. That is, what works particularly well for one student may be totally inappropriate for another. Read this section as a stimulus or springboard for your own experimentation. If you find one approach lacking, then vary your notetaking technique and try again. You will eventually find a system which is right for you. As a platform from which to spring, let's look at the following topics: lecture format; lecture organisational patterns; irrelevancies, and delivery cues. Some practical suggestions for actual notetaking will follow these sections.

Lecture format

Most tertiary lectures will have three basic parts: an introduction; the body or major points of the lecture; and it is hoped, a summary at the end, if the lecturer has not run overtime, which many are in the habit of doing.

The introduction is vital. Unfortunately, many students are often late and miss the first part of lectures. Why is the introduction so important? Generally, a good lecturer will attempt to present an overview of the topic, the aim and the rationale for the topic and the particular approach. Very astute lecturers will also link the themes of the preceding lectures to the present topics. The brief review will help to get you mentally primed and ready. Thus, get to the lecture on time, get settled and get ready to *think* and write. Remember, listening and notetaking are *active* mental processes and you must be ready to work when you enter the lecture hall.

The body, of the lecture will vary according to the approach of the lecturer and the nature of the lecture material. Generally, the lecturer will be trying to establish several points and then provide examples and illustrative material to support these points.

Undoubtedly, you will meet some very good lecturers, many average or mediocre ones and, unfortunately, a few who are hopelessly poor communicators. I look back with fondness upon one of my early university lecturers who was a bundle of nerves every lecture. Dr X was the archetypal dishevelled and absent-minded university professor. He would stumble onto the podium, shuffle his papers, half strangle himself with the neck microphone and then proceed to make a general mess of the lecture. I am certain he was hired because of his impressive research capabilities and his scholarly publications, but speak publicly he could not. Fortunately, he was a most endearing person and his students accepted his bewildering lectures as a cognitive challenge. The informal criterion for a pass in his course was simply making some sense of his lectures. Thank goodness, many tertiary institutions now encourage teaching staff to improve their communication skills with in-service training. Some institutions even give special recognition to particularly proficient lecturers, a positive inducement to staff to improve their skills.

Let's hope the majority of your lecturers will be competent. With attentive and active listening and some selective notetaking, you should be able to listen and profit from their presentations. If they are good lecturers, their presentations should terminate in a summary. However, these concluding remarks are often missed by some students, generally the ones who were late for the start of the lecture. Typically, these students clap their notebooks shut and dash for the exit at the first mention of: In summary, ...

Just as the introduction is very important, the summary is a prime opportunity to check that you have the key points of the lecture. It is also the time when lecturers may make suggestions about other readings, examinable points and perhaps important announcements about associated work, such as essay assignments or lab reports. Stem the temptation to join the delinquents dashing for the doors. Stay put and make certain that your notes are comprehensive and compatible with the lecturer's summarising statements.

Lecture organisational patterns

You will find that your lectures vary considerably in their organisational patterns, but for convenience let's look at three categories: didactic, discursive and mixed.

The didactic lecture will be presented in a fairly straightforward manner with the major points delivered unambiguously. Many science and technology-based courses will follow a didactic format. For example, a biochemistry lecture on the Kreb's cycle would probably follow the cycle step-by-step in an orderly fashion so that students grasped the sequential energy relationships. In other disciplines, any lecture topic which has lists of characteristics or systematic and orderly relationships is best presented in a didactic format. However, this is not to say that some free-thinking and alternative-minded teaching staff might not want to teach a scientific concept in perhaps a poetic fashion. There could be some scope, perhaps, for forest ecology to be taught partially from the writings of Thoreau at Walden Pond, but this would be the exception rather than the rule.

While the science, engineering and technology students can sit back somewhat comfortably in didactic lectures, the arts, humanities and social science students face a more difficult situation—discursive lectures. Metaphorically speaking, the discursive lecture might appear to students to be like a plate of spaghetti—intertwining concepts smothered by a sauce of fuzzy philosophising. Filtering out the key concepts can be just as challenging as eating spaghetti free from noodle whiplash. One helpful word of advice: prior to lectures, do the pre-reading suggested earlier to gain an orientation to the lecture topics. That small investment in time and energy will help considerably in sorting the essentials from the waffle.

The last organisational style is the mixed format. Probably the bulk of your lectures will be mixed and have both didactic and discursive elements. Your job will be sifting and sorting to glean the essence. Keep your mind tuned to the main points of the lecture and ask yourself repeatedly: Is this important? If so, how? These two questions will assist you to get the major topics onto your notepad.

Irrelevancies

Good lecturers will lighten the lecture with various bits of irrelevancy. For example, you might hear a short personal report about the last weekend, a joke or two, an anecdote, a quip from the news or an occasional comment about the institution's food. These comments and reports are obviously not key topics for notetaking, even though Molly who was discussed earlier felt compelled to get every syllable recorded on her notepad. The irrelevant parts of your lectures are good opportunities to have a short break and to rest your active writing hand. However, do not get too relaxed, as the lecturer should certainly return to the central issues following the light relief. Remember, notetaking is active and hard work, both mentally and physically.

Delivery cues

Just as body language is very important in managing well your work and home relationships, the same cues can be critical in extracting the key points in lectures. The cues which you should carefully observe are vocal variations (tone, speed and volume), postural changes (learning forward), gestures (using fingers and hand signals), and visual fixations (firm eye contact with the class). Good lecturers will use a variety of body language cues to emphasise key points as well as to increase the interest value of the lecture. Poor lecturers may drone on in a monotone and bore students to sleep, presenting a very special challenge for the keen notetaker.

Let's look at an example. Imagine that during a class, the lecturer paused, looked up and around the class and waited for several seconds before proceeding with the next point. How would you interpret this brief break in the lecture? The pause might suggest, *Get that down in your notes. It's an examinable point.* On the contrary, the pause might also mean that the lecturer has lost a thought or two and is searching for a link with which to proceed. Your interpretation of the various cues will be contingent upon the context in which they occur. Interpreting these cues can be challenging, but do monitor the lecturer's body language to gain maximal value from the lecture.

A psychology professor whom I shall call Dr Y was particularly adept at using delivery cues, but his performance was marred by one idiosyncrasy—he habitually paced from one extreme on the elevated podium to the other, returning to the central lectern when he had to consult his notes. The class of about twenty students decided to experiment upon poor Dr Y using an operant conditioning technique. We agreed to look up with firm interest and attentive smiles whenever he strayed from the lectern and then to look down, appearing bored and even occasionally yawning when he went back to the lectern. As Dr Y progressed through the lecture he was obviously responding to our cues. The high, or should I say low point of the lecture came when he was straying widely to the right on the podium. He was evidently reluctant to quickly return to the lectern to check his notes as he might get yawned at even more. While lost in thought about the next point, he toppled off the right side of the podium. The class was greatly amused. Fortunately, Dr Y was unhurt and a good sport. He congratulated the class on a prize prank when the conditioning procedure was explained.

Practical notetaking strategies

In order to get the most out of your lectures, try the following suggestions for notetaking.

- Record the name of the lecturer, the date and title of the lecture at the top of the first page. Number and date the following pages in case your notebook is dropped and the notes blow around.

- Leave plenty of open space on each page so that you can record extra notes and comments later.

- Take special note of diagrams, graphs and charts which are used during the lecture. If you do not have sufficient time to draw a facsimile, be certain to get the general theme so that you can record the details later.

- For lectures in which complex diagrams from the text are frequently used, take your text along to class so you can consult it during the lecture.

- Try to establish the lecturer's style early in the lecture, but be flexible and adaptable.

- If you are being distracted by students chatting nearby, change your seat or ask them to be quiet.

- Try to organise your notes as you listen. Many students find outlining and numbering the main points to be helpful.

- Avoid re-writing your notes. It's simply a very time-expensive task, and time will be in very short supply. Train your ears, eyes, mind and hand to get the essence plus important details down on your notepad.

- Use highlighters, coloured pens and other equipment to make the important headings and details stand out.

- Should ancillary notes be needed, write them on separate sheets and tape them to the relevant page. Try to have all of your notes pertaining to a particular topic located on the same page.

Two further points are worthy of special comment. Many students think that a portable tape recorder is the answer to their notetaking worries. With current recorders, it is perfectly possi ble to obtain a reasonable recording of a lecture if you sit near the front of the class. However, tape recording of lectures without the permission of the lecturer is generally frowned upon. Apart from getting the lecturer's permission, it is important to ask yourself how you are going to use the recording. You will quickly find that re-playing a tape from a one hour lecture will probably take at least ninety minutes. Inevitably, you will use the stop, pause or replay facilities to check on points and clarify your notes. The best approach is to perfect your listening and note-taking skills so that you do not have to spend these protracted periods with your tape recorder. Should you be ill or miss a few lectures for other reasons, then listening to a tape is certainly recommended, but do not depend upon lecture recordings as the answer to notetaking problems. Improving your listening and notetaking skills is a far more efficient approach.

The second issue relates to personal notetaking conventions, abbreviations or hieroglyphics, if your writing style is particularly unconventional. In many courses you will use the same terminology over and over. Rather than write out cumbersome terms repeatedly, develop a suitable abbreviation. However, be sure to note the meanings of your abbreviations (eg. PSYN = photosynthesis) so that the notes are meaningful to you later. While speaking about abbreviations, you might want to consider some standard terms which have been used by many students.

Sample of some notetaking symbols are shown on the next page.

Following the lecture

Many students leave the lecture hall and on returning home, stash their lecture notes in a file. This file remains shut until the next test or exam is imminent. Regrettably, most students allow insufficient time to revise their notes prior to examinations. Reading over your notes in a panicky state in the final week or two before your exams is a very poor substitute for systematic week-by-week learning. However, most part-time students will quickly respond that there is little or no time for learning notes prior to this pre-exam panic period. Even though time is scarce, there is a better way of dealing with your lecture notes so that learning is maximised.

→ LEADS TO, CAUSES, DIRECTION	
↑ INCREASE, MUCH, ELEVATE, HIGH	
↓ DECREASE, DESCEND, LOW, LITTLE, FEW	
↔ BOTH WAYS, EITHER WAY	
= EQUAL	≠ UNEQUAL
≃ APPROXIMATELY	Δ CHANGE
∴ THEREFORE	+ ADD TO, PLUS
♂ MALE, ⊙♂ FATHER	− TAKE AWAY, SUBTR
♀ FEMALE, ⊙♀ MOTHER	÷ DIVIDE
ϕ BIRTH	× TIMES, MULTIPLY
† DEATH	@ AT, EACH
⇒ IMPLIES	& AND
∵ BECAUSE	c̄ WITH
B/W BETWEEN	~ ABOUT
> GREATER THAN	WRT WITH RESPECT T
< LESS THAN	

<u>SUBJECT-SPECIFIC ABBREVIATIONS</u>

EEG ELECTROENCEPHALOGRAPH

GNP GROSS NATIONAL PRODUCT, ETC.

Studies on short-term memory have shown that there is about an 80 per cent decay in retention of lecture material within 24 hours. Thus, you will have little chance of recalling more than about twenty per cent of the details of a lecture you attended yesterday, unless of course you revised your notes in the meantime. The best way to preserve the key concepts and associated details in your memory is to review your lecture notes periodically. Studies have shown that the first revision should occur as soon as possible following the lecture and then another revision within the following few days with several weekly revisions thereafter. Yes, that's a lot of work, but if you want to keep anything in your memory, you will have to work hard.

If you have a few minutes following your lectures, stay in your seat and run your eyes over your notes. If you missed any critical points or did not understand a concept, you can ask the lecturer at this time. Later, when you return home, read your lecture notes more carefully. If there are major points of omission or areas of confusion, refer to a relevant text and make some additional notes. Tape these supplementary notes to a border of your original note sheet, forming a flap which can be folded out for revision.

Having worked through your lecture notes and supplemented them where necessary, you should now have a firm foundation to work with over the remainder of the academic term. The care and scrutiny which you give your notes at this point is very important, as learning is generally far easier when the concepts are clearly and concisely noted. Thus, the time invested at day's end will provide bountiful profits in the weeks ahead, especially during the pre-exam revision period.

Weekend revision of notes

In order to maintain your active recall of lecture concepts, reserve several hours at the end of each week to systematically revise the week's lectures. Take several hours on Saturday or Sunday morning to revise your week's notes from each subject. Yes, it is valuable time to sleep, shop, clean or fix, but question your priorities. Is it better to thrive in my studies and further my career or have, for example, a sparkling clean house? Your long term outlook should argue strongly for the work/study alternatives.

Having revised your notes several times, try to use the information in class discussions or even conversations at work and at home. As you know, commonly used telephone numbers are stored and easily retrieved from your mind. While your lecture topics will differ radically from telephone numbers, the principle is the same. Using information helps you to learn it. However don't bore your colleagues and family members by repeatedly introducing academic and esoteric topics into mealtime conversation. Your classmates may be more receptive and responsive in the academic milieu.

One final comment about your notes and exams. When you are revising your notes, keep a pen in hand and jot down the key terms on scratch paper to test yourself. If you can't record the essence of what you have just read in your notes, then you probably don't know the material well enough. Don't be lured into a false sense of security, thinking you have a rock hard knowledge of your notes when in reality you have but a handful of sand. The tensions of the exam room are prone to cause fine sand to filter between your fingers leaving you with little if any residue. Keep going over your notes until your knowledge is as firm and hard as granite. For further information about preparation for your examinations, read *How to pass exams* by F.E. Orr.

Checklist

( ) I listen actively rather than just hear.

( ) I pre-read relevant sources before lectures to prime my mind about key topics.

( ) I sit in the front of the class when possible to minimise distractions.

( ) I tune my listening to the style of the lecturer and the format of the presentation.

( ) I am aware of body language and listen with my ears and my eyes.

( ) I leave my classes with the best set of notes possible.

( ) I revise my class notes within 24 hours.

Summary

This chapter has described the important tasks of listening actively and effectively in lectures and taking lecture notes. The following points were discussed in detail:

- Listen actively during your lectures, don't just hear. Be alert, active and attuned to the messages of the lecturer.
- Have a syllabus for each subject being studied and prepare for each lecture by skimming the suggested readings.
- Be aware of the lecture format and style of organisation. Use the introduction to warm up, focus upon getting the central issues from the body of the lecture, and check on the completeness of your notes during the summarising remarks.
- Remain flexible by adapting to the lecturer's changes from didactic to discursive or to a mixed lecture style.
- Do not become distracted by the irrelevancies presented in the lectures.
- Monitor closely the various delivery cues used by the lecturer.
- Use abbreviations to make your notetaking more efficient and effective.
- Follow-up your lectures with systematic revision of your notes, both daily and weekly, to enhance your learning.
- Be certain that your revision for exams is well underway early in the term rather than just before your exams.

4
Reading more effectively

- *The theory of speed reading*
- *Speed reading exercises*
- *Analytical reading*
- *Skim reading*
- *Repetition reading of lecture notes*
- *Scanning reference materials*
- *Critical reading and editing*

Mark finished his university degree with first class honours in education, but after a brief exposure to the rigours and stress of teaching overly-exuberant teenagers, he decided to change his career. Having invested years of study into education, he made a radical move—into the business world as a trainee in a management consultancy firm.

Walking into this new career area was a shock and the job remained an interesting but persistent challenge. Within 18 months of starting, Mark was lured away by a merchant bank to a position in their international securities department. He was flattered by the offer and excited by the position. However, in calmer moments the excitement could well be described as unabashed fear, as Mark had no experience with international securities. The new job involved a full day of work (at the desk soon after 7am!) and three evenings of lectures. Time was extremely limited and keeping abreast of the reading and studying was going to be a Herculean challenge.

This chapter will present several different reading approaches which Mark used to conquer his reading problems both at work and study. Because time is limited for most part-time students, the chapter will focus particularly upon the study sector—how to get the most value from your reading time.

As a starter in reading efficiency, skim this chapter (glance down each page looking for relevant topics) and note the issues which have practical significance. Then go back and read with the purpose of learning more about how these skills will help you.

The theory of speed reading

Most conscientious students and business people have considered
taking a speed reading course. I was no exception. Prior to
starting university, I spent three weeks in a study-skills program.
I struggled and laboured on a reading rate accelerator for two
hours each day trying to keep ahead of a black screen which
progressed down the page at a set rate. Those hours of toil and
tension will never be forgotten. The descending screen was an
ever-present threat. My concentration was broken by fleeting
thoughts: Should I cut my losses and jump down to the next
paragraph; or, should I press ahead at the screen's edge? Having
battled through the reading exercise, I was then expected to
answer questions to test my comprehension. The experience was
nothing short of gruelling, but the results were not so grim.

Despite the tension generated on the reading accelerator, my
speed did increase about three fold after the intensive training. I
started the program reading about 350 words per minute and
finished at just over the 1000 mark.

You might well be wondering how the process of reading
acceleration works and, more specifically, how you can become a
more rapid reader. The answer is likely to be disappointing—
consistent practice! Unfortunately, there are very few miracles
and instant answers in the study arena. If you are not too discouraged by that news, then read on to learn more about the process
of reading acceleration.

The essence of becoming a more rapid reader involves expand-
ing your visual field. The process does not involve a stretching
exercise in the muscular sense. It's more a process of widening
your visual field and concentrating very hard on your reading
matter.

Basically, we read by fixing our eyes on the words or syllables
of the reading matter which allows an impression to be made
upon the retinas of our eyes. When reading a typical newspaper
column, you might have four to eight eye fixations as you move
your eyes across the column of newsprint, depending upon the
number and length of the words. Each fixation takes only a
fraction of a second, but all those bits of time add up when
reading lengthy works. The secret of speed reading is to reduce

the number of eye fixations and therefore reduce the overall amount of time necessary to read the material. Sounds very simple and straightforward, but it is certainly a matter of hard work.

Speed reading exercises

Try reading a column of newsprint by fixing your eyes only twice in each line. It's difficult, but certainly possible. You just have to break free from your old reading habits in which you have been lingering too long on each line. Try to resist the temptation to read each word individually. The ultimate challenge, of course, is to move your eyes straight down the middle of each column and absorb the essence of the material along that line and on both sides.That takes strong concentration, firm discipline, plus a very absorbent mind.

While your eyes are moving down the column, your mind should be extremely active. Ask yourself continually: Is this relevant? If so, how? Look for key words, italicised terms, bold face print, and sub-headings. These terms will guide you in sifting the topical material from the trivial. Your mind will need to work very actively, but with practice, your reading speed will increase appreciably.

Having practised the technique, you might find that you have indeed read faster, but your understanding of the material might be poor. High reading speed without adequate comprehension is certainly not going to win you high praise at work or high marks in your examinations.

In order to check your comprehension, read an article using the technique described above. Next, write down the general theme and the five most important points in the article. Reread the article more slowly and carefully and check your comprehension. Did you misunderstand the theme? Did you pick up the important points? If your comprehension was poor, you may want to slow down your reading speed to increase your comprehension. With practice, however, your speed will increase with little or no decrease in comprehension. But, it will take a lot of practice.

In order to increase your speed and reading comprehension, try to spend, say, fifteen minutes each day speed reading. A prime practice time is when you read the morning newspaper. Move your eyes quickly down the columns and absorb the key terms and general meaning. You will be keeping abreast of the news and increasing your reading speed concurrently. You will also experience the positive feeling of having accomplished a set task before you have even left for work.

Practise at other times on leisure and recreational reading. As a reminder to read more quickly and wisely, make a mental note to *read rapidly* whenever you pick up a book or magazine. That mental message should push you out of the slow and slogging word-to-word reading into a more efficient reading pace. Keep practising and you will certainly experience an increase in your reading rate.

In summary, try to reduce the number of eye fixations as you read across the page by stretching your visual field. Keep your mind very alert and very active by asking yourself: 'Is this relevant? If so, how?' Be certain to test your comprehension periodically to make certain that you are getting the major points from your reading. The most important point in accelerating your reading speed is to practise regularly, say fifteen minutes each day. After several months of practice, your reading rate will increase.

Analytical reading

While speed reading is certainly recommended for leisure reading, many students might be justifiably hesitant about speed reading their textbooks. They are likely to fear that they will not pick up the essential details. If you are reading to understand thoroughly and learn the material, you will need to read in a different way. The method to be described is called the SQ3R technique. The acronym stands for: Survey, Question, Read, Recite, Review. Let's look at each of these stages individually.

Survey the material

Prior to any systematic reading, leaf through the pages and mentally survey the chapter or section which you intend to read. Keep a pen in hand and as you run your eye down each page, note on paper any major terms in bold face print or italics. Take special notice of graphs, charts and other visual aids. They have been put into the book to assist your comprehension of the concepts being discussed. The survey process should only take a few minutes and at the end of this time you should have a list of terms or concepts noted on paper.

Question the meaning and significance of terms

Look over the list of terms and concepts which you have noted during your survey of the reading material. Try to formulate a question about each noted term. For example, if you have just surveyed a chapter on photosynthesis, you might have various terms such as chlorophyll, solar energy, light reaction and dark reaction listed on your note paper. Ask yourself, Chlorophyll— function? Solar energy—role? The questions do not have to be lengthy. In fact, just the key word, such as chlorophyll followed by a question term such as *role*?; *chemistry*? would suffice to prompt goal-directed reading.

Goal-directed reading means that you read specifically to find answers to your questions. Research studies have shown that work done for a specific purpose will tend to be more efficient than work done without specified goals. In addition to improving the efficiency of your reading and comprehension, the survey and question steps serve to warm up your mind to the more detailed reading to follow. It's much like doing some warm up exercises prior to a vigorous workout—our bodies function better, mind and muscles alike, when they are appropriately prepared.

Read the material

Having surveyed the chapter and noted questions, it is now time to read the material. While the reading is meant to be a significant learning process, that does not necessarily mean it has to be slow. Try to move your eyes as quickly as you can over the lines, searching for the crucial terms and concepts. Try not to pause on common words. For example, there is no benefit in pausing on words like: the, a, but and other articles, prepositions or conjunctions. Save your time and mental energy for the major terms and concepts.

You will find a pen to be a very handy and helpful memory device. Keep a pen in your hand and when you come upon critical terms, underline them (if the book belongs to you) or make a note on scratch paper. Don't take copious and lengthy notes (that's very time expensive), just the key terms. Learning is an *active* process and the more activity you can put into it, the more you will retain. Having read a section and made some brief notes, you are now ready for the next step—recite.

Recite the major points

Recitation is a verbal recounting of the major points you have just read. Having finished a section of reading, perhaps five or ten paragraphs, pause and look up. Ask yourself, What are the three to five most important points in the section I have just read? Then, recite the points ... That should be reasonably simple, if you have been attentive.

While the process appears quite simple and straightforward, there are possible snags. Every student will recall many occasions when reading was replaced by daydreaming, dozing or dawdling. The occasional mental lapse is normal, but regular concentration breaks can cost the student valuable time.

The recitation phase of the SQ3R process functions partly as a quality control step. You pause briefly in the reading process and assess the quality of your reading. If you cannot recite the major points of the material you have just read, then go back over it. There is generally little sense in pressing ahead if you are not understanding the basics.

To summarise, recitation is best done after reading short sections. Pause and mentally recite the major points. To help fix these ideas in your mind, use your pen to tick the points on the question sheet or make some brief additional notes. Ultimately though, the material will have to be lodged in your mind, not just on paper.

Review the material periodically

As mentioned in the preceding chapter, your short term memory is vulnerable to decay at a surprising rate. Eighty percent of what we mentally absorb will decay within twenty-four hours. How many of us would choose to enter an examination room with only about twenty per cent retention of a single reading of our lecture notes? Very few.

How can we deal with this mental decay of facts, figures, terms and concepts? By periodic review. The first review should take place immediately after reading the section. As you proceed, periodically review the previous sections so that you build up a comprehensive understanding of the material being read and learned. Following the initial reading, try to review the material briefly within twenty-four hours to foster greater retention. The review sessions can take only several minutes, but the repetition will significantly enhance your retention.

In summary, the SQ3R technique is a very systematic and *active* reading process which will improve your reading retention. Survey the material to gain an overview and warm up your mind to the task. Formulate brief questions about the prominent terms and concepts to establish goals for your reading. Read the first section of the material. Pause and mentally recite the major points. Then progress through the other sections, but pause periodically for brief reviews. Yes, it does take a bit of time and bother, but the research reports on this reading technique strongly support its efficacy.

Skim reading

Skim reading is the educational equivalent of skimming the cream off full bodied milk—you take the rich bit and leave the rest. That is precisely the task for the harried student. You want to get the central concept, but not get bogged down with illustrative matter and copious detail.

Skim reading is best used when you want to cover a large amount of reading matter in a little time. For example, a reading list of twenty books will look foreboding to most students, but the effective skim reader may well be able to attack the list and distil its contents in several hours. How can this be done? Read on (rapidly!)

One technique which skim readers use is to read the first and last two or three paragraphs of each chapter. The theory underlying this approach is that well written books generally present their messages at least three times: firstly in the introductory section; then in the body of the chapter; and once again in the summary. By reading the first and last paragraphs, you have a two in three chance of picking up the major themes and important concepts.

A second approach is to read only the first sentence of each paragraph. This technique will generally require more time, but it may be preferable to the previous approach, especially when reading more detailed material. For example, if you are studying photosynthesis and want to appraise the views of another writer on the same topic, reading the lead sentence of each paragraph will give you a more clear understanding of the writer's reasoning and argument than reading only the introduction and summary.

The lead sentence technique might also be preferable when reading a novel in a short period of time. I hasten to say that this technique is an insult to the artistry of the novelist who toiled over the choice of each word in the book, but when time is critical, word-by-word reading is a luxury few students can afford. A word of caution is important here. Even though you are short-circuiting the book, your mind will have to be very alert and incisive. While textbooks are generally written in a logically developed style, novels and other fictional works can be more difficult to read by a formula approach. However, that is not to say you should not try. To stay particularly alert, once again keep a pen in hand and jot down notes when appropriate. In novel reading, you will certainly want to note the prevailing themes and conflicts, the central plots, and the important characters.

Discuss the skimmed book with a classmate to improve your understanding and enhance your appreciation of the important points. This assumes, of course, that the other student read the book in equal or more detail.

In summary, skim reading is a technique which you can employ to get the central ideas of a chapter, book or article. Ask yourself which skimming technique is likely to offer the better outcome—first and last paragraphs or the lead sentence approach. Which ever technique is used, keep your mind very alert and your concentration at peak performance. Writing brief notes will help distil the themes from the text.

Repetition reading of lecture notes

While this topic was discussed briefly in the last chapter, some readers may have skimmed the material or skipped it altogether. If you have a sound understanding about revising your lecture notes, then move on to the next section.

Many students make the academically fatal mistake of reading their lecture notes only once or twice before entering the examination room. As they page through their notes, it all seems familiar and they become lured into a false sense of security.

How can you develop a rock hard knowledge of your lecture notes? By frequent and repeated readings of your notes. Ideally, this should be done on a weekly basis. Reserve some time each week to do nothing other than review your lecture notes. Try to think of these revision sessions as preparation time for an exam in the subject the following week. When you first go through your notes, they might well seem perplexing. However, as you review the notes several times, the fog will lift and perhaps you will gain a crystal clear understanding of the concepts.

Try to read through your notes rapidly the first few times. You will undoubtedly think you are not gaining very much from these cursory readings, but you will begin to pick up associations and relationships between concepts which only one slow reading would not generally develop.

In order to make the revision more lucid, keep a pen in your hand and jot down brief and quick notes to test yourself as you progress. Remember, the more active you can make your learning experiences, the more reliable will be your memory. If you can discuss your class notes with a friend, so much the better. Much like telephone numbers which you use frequently, the class notes which are read frequently and used in discussions will become part of your long term memory.

Scanning reference materials

When conducting reference research for assignments, students often spend too much time browsing through books of only marginal relevance. Your job is to get to the critical books quickly and then extract the relevant bits.

A basic and essential skill for efficient reference researching is knowing your library very well. If you are in doubt about your library skills, then ask a librarian to teach you how to conduct library research. Assuming that you either have the requisite library skills or will soon acquire them, let's press on with the scanning technique.

When you find an apparently relevant title on the library shelves, go immediately to the table of contents. Resist the temptation to just open the book randomly and start browsing. For part-time students, time is at a premium and you do not have time to waste with random reading. Look down the contents page searching for relevant chapters. If you do not see any topical listings, turn to the index and scan the items for relevant topics or key names. If neither the contents nor index provide any possible leads, then put the book back straight away and proceed with your research.

When you see a relevant chapter on the contents page, go directly to the chapter's first page. Read the first paragraph or two looking for some statement about the contents of the chapter. If the introductory paragraphs do not seem to have anything directly relevant, page quickly to the end of the chapter and read the final several paragraphs. If nothing pops up in the summary, go directly to the next chapter on your list. Do *not* get enticed into reading bits of the chapter because it is generally interesting. Your job is much more specific—to get the researching done and then get to your writing. Time is limited, especially precious library time for part-time students, so keep up the pace and maximise your efficiency.

Let's say that you do see a reference to the topic you are researching in the first paragraph of a chapter. Page quickly through the chapter to where the topic is discussed in more detail. Skim read the lead sentences of the paragraphs until you come to the critical part. Then, and only then, should you read more specifically. Find the relevant bits, take some brief notes if warranted, and then move onto the next reference. The motto for good reference researchers is: get to the library; get the reference sources; get the essence; and then get out and to the writing.

At this point it is pertinent to mention the lure of the photo-copying machines. Many students who are pressed for time will spend many valuable minutes and perhaps more valuable cents feeding these machines. Generally, students overuse the photo-copying machines because they feel insecure in their knowledge about their assignment topic. Given the difficulty in getting to the library on a part-time student's schedule, they often want to have the reference material in front of them when they commence writing, just in case they need further information.

Why not save some time and money by scanning the material and making a decision to either note it or leave it? Making these decisions can take courage, but a decisive and determined approach is likely to foster a more efficient research effort.

To summarise then, scanning is a helpful technique when doing library research. Make full use of the table of contents and book indices for possible leads and information sources. Don't become distracted by fascinating, but irrelevant material. When you come upon a chapter which appears relevant, find the essence as quickly as possible by skimming through the paragraphs. Resist the temptation to photocopy the chapter or selected bits. You will still have to read the material and possibly take notes, so standing in the queue and feeding the machine is only going to deplete you of time and money.

Critical reading and editing

Critical reading is used to judge or evaluate written material. Editing differs in that you read then alter the text or manuscript.

Critical reading is usually slow and laborious as you should be questioning and challenging the presented ideas. Given that the reading process is going to be slower than the other techniques described earlier, it is best to approach the reading chore with sufficient time and patience to do the job well. If you want to extract the themes and their underlying support, then read with pen in hand to note the relevant issues on paper. Any student of logic will agree that understanding a complex argument can be facilitated by noting the parts, the propositions and the supporting evidence. Don't try to mentally outmanoeuvre the philosophers—pen and paper are necessary tools if you are seriously interested in criticising the arguments in a complex manuscript.

Editing is a very valuable reading technique, especially if you are editing your own work. It is often said that good writing is good re-writing. What goes on during these re-writes is a lot of editing—chopping and changing.

All too often students procrastinate and try to write major essays and reports just before submission day. Because time is limited, they turn in the first draft or a rapidly read and fleetingly corrected second draft. At best, the prominent spelling and grammatical mistakes may have been picked up and corrected, but errors in syntax and logic are rarely addressed in these eleventh hour rush jobs.

The essential feature in editing is to allow sufficient time to pass for maturation of your ideas. What looks very acceptable today may well look ludicrous tomorrow. Ideally, plan for the editing to occur over several days. Read the report from start to finish each day, making corrections as you go. The ideal way to do this is on a word processor. If you do not have several days for editing, then plan to lose an hour or so of sleep and get up early. It is far preferable to edit the manuscript after you have slept rather than do it immediately after completing the initial draft.

Editing is a most demanding job. To do the job very well, every word should be considered for spelling, grammar and syntax: Is this the best possible word for the meaning and measure of the work?. If you are editing a handwritten report, then alterations are best added in pencil, just in case you decide to change again tomorrow. Some writers use a different colour of ink for each editing, but plenty of open space between lines is necessary to make this convention work well.

To check for 'tightness' in your writing, look at each paragraph and ask what relation it bears to its section heading, if section headings are being used. A secondary test is to question the relevance of each paragraph to the general thesis of the work. Yes, this does take time and patience, but as the saying goes: Rome wasn't built in a day.

Thus, critical reading and editing are both slow and meticulous processes. Time will be needed for both. When reading the manuscript, it is necessary to think carefully about flow of ideas and the logic of relationships. If errors are discovered, then you either note them or correct them, depending upon your function —to criticise or to edit.

Checklist

( ) I adjust my reading speed and style to the material being read.
( ) I practise speed reading on leisure reading matter.
( ) I try to skim over unimportant words such as articles, prepositions and conjunctions and look for key nouns and verbs.
( ) I read and then revise several times material which must be learned.
( ) I use skimming and scanning techniques when conducting library research.

Summary

Reading is one of the most basic, important and time consuming functions of students. This chapter has described the following reading issues and techniques, including a brief overview of speed reading.

- *Speed reading*
  Train your eyes to stop less often in each line and to widen their field of view. Practise daily with the morning newspaper to increase your reading speed.
- *Reading techniques*
  Analytical reading—Use the Survey, Question, Read, Recite, Review technique to enhance your comprehension.

  Skim reading—Read the first and last paragraphs of a chapter or the lead sentence in each paragraph depending upon the type of reading being done.

Reading of lecture notes—Review your lecture notes as soon as possible after each lecture. Reserve several hours each week to do nothing other than reading and learning your lecture notes. Study your notes with a pen in hand to test your own understanding.

Scanning of reference sources—Use the Contents and Index to guide you to the essential parts of the book. Scan the beginning and ends of chapters to survey the key topics. Exercise restraint at reading interesting, but unrelated bits, as time is at a premium.

Critical reading and editing—Read meticulously to understand and assess the arguments and structure of the manuscript. Use notes to disentangle complex arguments. Ensure you have several days if editing your own work, as it will always look a bit different tomorrow.

5
Sharpening your information research skills

- **Time traps in the library**
- **Time savers in library research**
- **General principles of efficient assignment research**

Veronica was fresh from the country and working as a clerk with a city bank while pursuing a commerce degree three evenings a week. She found city life to be overpowering at first and she experienced very similar feelings when she first attended the university. When first visiting the university library, Veronica felt inadequate and perplexed as she was uncertain about how to use the services and facilities. Just getting her bearings from the library map was a challenge.

Even though Veronica excelled in her high school work and thought she knew how to use a library, she quickly discovered that the university library was in a very different league. When she entered the library to pursue her first research assignment in Economic History, she did not know where and how to start.

As any resourceful student would do, Veronica went directly to the reader's assistance desk for help. In order to learn how to use the new facilities, she registered for a library orientation course and then proceeded to get started on her assignment.

During her years of evening study, Veronica developed skills which helped her cope with the difficult situation of most part-time students—getting to the library during the open hours and making efficient use of her research time when there. You might well profit from some of the strategies Veronica developed during her years as a part-time student.

This chapter will discuss how you can become more effective and efficient when researching in the library. Following a presentation of some common time traps, various time saving strategies will be presented. A comprehensive description of library skills goes beyond the scope of this book, but you can receive some helpful information by contacting your university librarians.

Time traps in the library

Veronica's initial apprehension when approaching the library for the first time will be familiar to many students. Even though most libraries make concerted efforts to be 'user friendly', just the size of the building and the perceived complexity of the equipment and facilities can be intimidating. It is very important for you to become competent, confident and efficient in your library research skills.

Most students, be they full or part-time, will initially fall into various library time traps. The most common traps are failure to know the basic operating procedures of the library; uncertainty about the library's geography; and inability to correctly operate the equipment.

It is unlikely that every student will be fully competent following an initial library orientation tour. The true learning will commence when you have your first assignment in hand and you start organising your information search. Rather than assume you now know how the system works, be prepared to consult the library staff so that your learning continues. Get a map, walk around the resource areas to get your bearings, use the catalogue system and other basic equipment. As mentioned in Chapter three of this book, using information prompts learning.

Mark, one of Veronica's classmates, was overly confident about his library skills and did not register for the orientation program. Consequently, when researching his first assignment, he wandered around the library stacks looking for books which, in fact, were not located there. He wasted time looking for one particular book which he later discovered was out on loan. His haphazard methods caused him sufficient annoyance that he eventually sought assistance. In addition to helping Mark organise his research efforts, the librarian also convinced him to join the next library orientation program.

Know your library's geography

As suggested in the cases of Veronica and Mark, the orientation program will teach you the library's geography and how to find your way to the various resources. During the library tour, you will be shown how to use the book borrowing system and the various reference areas. You will also learn how to operate the research equipment, such as microfiche machines and photocopiers. You will undoubtedly be informed about the penalties for not getting your borrowed books back on time. There is, after all, a limit to how far the friendliness of the library can extend.

To continue learning about the library's geography and basic services, keep a careful eye on the signs, posters, bookmarks and any other information media used to keep library users abreast of new developments.

Time savers in library research

Most part-time students will be fighting a continual battle against the clock. Work duties, class lectures and private study will account for a large amount of your time, leaving very little for research activities in the library. The challenge will be to find time to get to the library and once there, to get your research done as quickly and effectively as possible. Try the following suggestions in order to become more time efficient in your library research.

- List your specific research goals for each trip to the library plus a realistic completion time. Enjoy the feeling of accomplishment as you cross the goals off your list as you accomplish them.
- Try to use the library facilities at off-peak times to minimise waiting in queues.
- Prior to arriving at the library, make a comprehensive list of related topics which need researching. Try to minimise return trips to the library just to tidy up loose ends.
- If you are unfamiliar with the research topic, ask a librarian for advice about general resources, such as annual reviews or topical yearbooks.
- Avoid garrulous classmates while conducting your library research. Socialising is best left to your leisure time.
- Before going to the bookshelves to look for your reference sources, check the loan list to see which books are unavailable.
- For books you deem to be crucial and which are out on loan, place an urgent recall request with the circulation librarian.

- When queues are long at the photocopier or circulation desk, come back later or start reading the reference material while standing and waiting.

- Use efficient reading techniques to skim and scan for pertinent resource material. Ask yourself while scanning: Is this useful? If so, how?

- Be sparing in your notetaking as notes are time expensive. When taking notes, be brief and concise.

- When recording a note, be sure to indicate where you think the note can be used in your assignment. Students are frequently mystified when they later read some library research notes, wondering how they could possibly use them.

- Get to know your classmates so that you can share resources. It is far more economical on everyone's time if you can arrange to work as a syndicate on major projects. One person can make the trip to the library and photocopy relevant material for a later syndicate meeting.

- When searching for books and materials which are hard to get, contact other local libraries or consider arranging an inter-library loan.

- Use the telephone before making a trip to the library to enquire about the availability of difficult to find resources. Librarians are generally willing to respond to occasional telephone requests in special circumstances.

Several of these time savers require organising other people. You will profit from these experiences in team coordination by saving library research time.

Researching at work

In addition to practising the above suggestions and becoming very efficient in the library, Veronica became skilled at pursuing some research activities while at work. This strategy may not be immediately applicable to every part-time student, but Veronica's approach is worth considering for present or future reference.

Veronica's time saving started before the academic year commenced. As she knew that time was going to be very tight,

Veronica selected course electives which had direct relevance to the work she was doing at the bank. One criterion she used in her subject selection was the range of assignment topics noted on the syllabus. She chose an economics elective which covered issues relevant to investment analysis, the bank department in which she worked. Thus some of her work time at the bank was doubly used for researching her essays. For example, she used the bank's data base scanning facility and obtained a comprehensive listing of all publications in the past ten years pertaining to one of her essay topics. She then checked the bank's library for appropriate resources and borrowed the relevant books. The course assignments were so closely aligned with Veronica's work that in one instance she was able to submit a copy of a major project to the department manager at the bank. As stated above, it is rare for such synchronisation to exist between part-time study and work duties, but the time savings are significant if the conditions are available. If this situation applies to you, choose your subjects carefully so that you too can make double use of some work and study time.

General principles for efficient assignment research

For those students who are not in the enviable position of using some work time for assignment research, there are some general guidelines which may help you to become more efficient in your research.

- Don't procrastinate. Start the assignment immediately.
- Establish weekly goals to keep your assignment progress up to date.
- Construct a tentative outline so you know what you will need to research.
- List your research goals before entering the library.
- Try to use the library at off-peak times to avoid long waits.
- When in doubt about your research assignment, consult the lecturer.
- When in doubt about how to get started or progress further with your information search, consult a librarian.

- Keep up to date on new facilities and services at the library.
- Share resources with other students. Work in syndicates to maximise efficiency.
- Establish a firm completion time for researching your assignment.
- Accept the fact that you will never know everything about the topic. Resist strongly the temptation to put off writing until you get every available detail. Start writing on your predetermined first draft date.

Thus, being disciplined and determined will assist you in getting your library research completed. Start your projects on time and work to a weekly schedule. Plan your research program and then implement it. Get to the library, get the information and then get to work on the drafting of the assignment. Maintaining an up-to-date knowledge about the library and the services available will enhance your efficiency in library research.

Checklist

( ) I have participated in a library orientation program.
( ) I keep abreast of new developments in the library.
( ) I ask librarians for assistance when I have been unsuccessful in solving a library research problem.
( ) I strive to save time by planning my research goals and by using library facilities in off-peak hours.
( ) I use the telephone to consult other information sources.
( ) I try to work in research syndicates so that the members can share resources.
( ) I organise my course electives so to overlap with my job responsibilities, if appropriate.

Summary

This chapter has discussed how to maximise your efficiency in researching your course assignments. The following topics were discussed:

- Participate in a library orientation program when first starting your course.

- Plan your project.
- Construct a tentative outline to help organise your information search.
- Get to the library early.
- Consider working in a syndicate to share resources.
- Consult librarians when necessary.
- Plan your library sessions for off-peak times to avoid long queues.
- Finish your reading/notetaking on schedule, leaving plenty of time for writing.

6

Writing research reports and essays

- *A systematic approach to report writing*
- *Establish a project file*
- *Set weekly goals*
- *Preliminary reading*
- *Preliminary outline*
- *Researching and notetaking*
- *Writing the first draft*
- *Redrafting*
- *Learning from returned assignments*

With the deadline of your next major assignment pressing, have you just decided that you had better get started on the preliminary steps? On reading the topic question and related materials, do you fail to understand exactly what the assignment is all about, but stagger ahead regardless, hoping that the issue will become clear? Do you experience bursts of anxiety when you think about the total number of words which must be written over the next days or weeks? Do you put off the initial drafting until you have read just another few references to be absolutely certain of your position? During the writing phase, do you get muddled with bits and pieces of paper on which you have written your notes? Finally, do you fail to get your assignment in on time?

For many part-time students who have been squeezing essay and report writing into their already frantic workdays, the situations noted above will be very familiar. Because your essays and reports count for a majority of your final course marks, you should conquer the skills of good report writing. Being an effective report writer is also a work skill much valued by employers. These are but two good reasons why you might read and then apply the helpful pointers that follow.

In this chapter you will learn how to prepare for major writing projects, from establishing a file on the subject and determining a realistic time plan to writing your final draft. The chapter will take you step by step through a systematic plan for organising, preparing and then writing your reports. The essence of the procedure is to start each project early and work through the stages systematically so that your final result is well-organised, thoroughly worked and submitted on time.

Jeremy was an apprentice cook who had various projects to complete on diet and nutrition. He thoroughly enjoyed working for a large international hotel. The hotel was thriving and he was often asked to work overtime to meet the pressing schedules of the kitchen. When a major writing assignment was due in the middle of one of these rush periods at work, the assignment often received short shrift.

Jeremy was often frustrated by the absence of resource books from the library shelves and by the absence of his instructors during their scheduled consultation hours. However, his major concern was a writing problem—finding some logical path through the assigned topic. We worked through the points discussed in this chapter to improve his report writing skillls. Perhaps the same points might be helpful to you as well.

A systematic approach to report writing

Many students dive straight into the writing of a report rather than give the topic adequate forethought and preparation. Try the following steps to establish a firm and logical approach to your writing assignments.

Establish a project file

When you are assigned a report topic, take the first step and establish a file. Use a manila folder for filing the assignment sheet and subsequent notes.

Record your early thoughts and ideas

As soon as possible after the project has been assigned, sit down and think about the topic. Make some notes about issues related to the central theme. Don't worry about quality at this stage. What you want is quantity of thoughts. You can sort the good from the poor later.

Set weekly goals

If you have the luxury of six weeks to prepare the assignment, don't wait for several weeks to get started. Start immediately and set weekly goals. The goals will differ with various projects, but for most major pieces of work, you should be able to divide the total task into a series of weekly sub-tasks. Consider the following schedule as a guide for a typical 3000 word assignment.

Week	Goals
1	Start file; set weekly goals; brainstorm topic; note ideas; clarify topic, if necessary
2	Preliminary reading; establish initial outline; notetaking
3	Further reading and research; notetaking; refine initial outline
4	Finalise outline and *start writing* by / / !
5	Complete inital draft; redraft and polish daily
6	Submit assignment on / /

The goals can be listed on a calendar or you can prepare a card for each project and cross off the separate goals as they are accomplished. Don't underestimate the value of actually crossing off the accomplished goals. That simple act is very rewarding. A list of crossed off goals fuels the creative and productive fires and keeps you moving ahead. It also acts as a visible and meaningful record of work accomplished, a most important aspect for students whose academic work is generally intangible and invisible.

Brainstorming the topic

In order to get started on the assignment, you will need to think widely about the topic. You should note a wide range of related ideas so that you can ultimately select a logically connected series to form the skeleton of your report. If the assigned topic is very general, such as 'The Sociology of the Family', you will want to narrow it considerably if you have a 3000 word limit.

Whether the topic is broad or specific, sit down and think about the topic and related issues for five minutes, three or four times over the next several days. Open the file and jot down your thoughts on a clean piece of paper during each brainstorming session. Look at the key terms in the question or topic to prompt your thinking. It might sound silly to open the file several times in one day for these five minute think-sessions, but you are a slightly different person each time. You want to approach the topic from a sound and sensible perspective and these brainstorming sessions may give you some practical leads.

Establish a firm understanding of the topic

Many essay topics will be totally new to you or they could be just confusing. Try to simplify the topic by breaking it down into parts. For example, if the topic is: 'Compare and contrast the economic theories of Marx and Keynes, with special reference to the national economic situation over the past five years' you will certainly want to research thoroughly Marxist and Keynesian theories. You will also need to decide which contemporary economic situations or phenomena you want to discuss in relation to the two theories.

If any of the terms in the topic are difficult to understand or if the wording of the question is ambiguous, then discuss the matter with your instructor. It is absolutely critical that you are precisely on target when you begin the assignment. Much like a transcontinental traveller, a $2-3°$ error at the beginning of the journey can put you well away from the final goal. So, be certain you know exactly what your target is right from the start and stay on target as you progress with the assignment.

For students whose course work relates to their paid employment, try to select projects which have some relevance to your job. Not only should the interest level be higher, but there could well be resources within the firm which could help with the assignment. For example, employees of the stock exchange would be well advised to select project topics which apply directly to the work of that organisation. As suggested in the preceding chapter, with job-related essay topics, you might then use your organisation's library or consult various resource people at work. Make the tough job of part-time study as easy as possible.

Preliminary reading

Many class research projects are selected because they are likely to challenge you. Given that you may not know very much about the assignment topic, you will have to do some preliminary research to establish a firm footing upon which to build your later research.

Your librarian should be able to help here. Ask about review journals or publications titled: Perspective on ..., or Advance in ... These publications are often more general in orientation and can serve to start you on your way. Your text book might have suggested readings at the end of relevant chapters which could also provide some good starting points for your research. Use the skimming and scanning techniques described in the preceding chapter to obtain a general overview. At this stage don't bother with a lot of notetaking; you just want to become familiar with the topic.

Preliminary outline

Having established some grounding in the topic, jot down several useful and relevant headings. Try to use the key words in the essay statement or derivative terms so that you keep closely on the topic.

If the preliminary outline looks like an insurmountable challenge for you, try the following approach. Ask a friend to sit and listen quietly while you present your early thoughts about the research topic. If you have a portable tape recorder, then record your presentation. Most students who try this technique are quite surprised to find that their commentary is generally relevant and logical. This positive flow of ideas in front of your friend probably occurs because of ego preservation. Having done some background reading and preliminary thinking about the topic, you will not want to appear to be dumb when you present your ideas. The very fact that someone is listening intently is often a sufficient push to get the ideas which are lurking in the dark shadows of your mind out into the daylight. Having the presentation tape, all you have to do is push the replay button and note the ideas

There is no guarantee that this will produce one hundred per cent results, but the technique has certainly unblocked the minds of many students.

Write a paragraph plan

Some students become intimidated by the length of their assignments. Sitting and worrying about the 5000 words which you are expected to produce is a considerable waste of time. Rather than fret over that formidable number, 5000, try the following approach.

Let's assume that your assignment is 5000 words and that your average paragraph length is about 100 words. That makes 50 paragraphs to complete the assignment, which doesn't sound nearly as bad as 5000 words, does it? Now, break the 50 paragraphs down into the various sections, as follows.

Sections	Paragraphs
Introduction	5
Body	
Concept A	10
Concept B	10
Concept C	10
Concept D	10
Summary/Conclusion	5
Total Paragraphs	50

The figures five and ten are far less threatening than the total word count, 5000. Numbers can have a very emotional effect, as any tax auditor will agree.

In addition to allaying fear, the paragraph plan also allows you to identify precisely where you plan to use the information you are noting during the researching and notetaking phases of the project.

Researching your topic

Learning how to research an essay or major report is a complex skill which challenges all new students. The previous chapter presented a range of skills for researching reports and essays. The present section will deal with some alternative sources of information.

- *Personal interviews.*
  Contact resource people and ask carefully-planned questions which will give you the information you want.
- *Newspaper files.*
  Telephone your local newspaper with requests for information which they might have on their files. This source will be more helpful when local issues are your research topic.
- *Questionnaire studies.*
  You can conduct your own appraisal of various issues by administering your own questionnaire to relevant groups. Consult an experienced questionnaire expert for advice about structuring your questions and selecting the sample.
- *Laboratory reports.*
  For scientific or technological topics, there might be reports which you, your colleagues or others have done in the laboratory which will relate to your research project.
- *Technical information supplied by companies.*
  Contact companies producing goods and services which relate to your topic. See the case studies below for further information.

Case Studies

Paul was in his final year of an engineering certificate at technical college and was employed as an administrative assistant in the engineering department of a local council. As part of his course, he asked permission to pursue a specific project—the applicability of concrete castings in the design of storm water drains, a topic which had obvious relevance to his job.

As he faced the same time constraints as other part-time students, Paul telephoned five major manufacturers of concrete castings and requested technical information on their products. Three of the firms sent technical representatives to discuss their products with Paul as well as to leave reams of information for his perusal. Paul had more up-to-date information than could have been provided by his technical college library.

Maureen was a third year part-time marketing student at university and a full-time clerk with the federal Department of Trade and Export. She requested a research topic on the overseas marketing of locally manufactured clothing. She was able to use the public service network to obtain the latest overseas marketing figures from the data bank within her department. The government statistician provided retrospective and prospective export figures. As you will guess, most of the research was done at work.

The message to be learned from these case studies is: try to make your course and your job as compatible as possible; and select essay and research topics which you can pursue at work. There should be absolutely no guilt from furthering your work and study objectives concurrently.

Notetaking

Taking notes from research sources is a very time expensive task. Because of limited opportunities to get to the library, many part-time students take excessive notes, just in case they need more information when they start writing. However, many of these notes go unused.

In a recent study, 28 students who were preparing a 3000 word essay in Economics I were asked to keep records of various activities during their project. All students were asked to calculate the average time spent taking notes during the reading and notetaking phases of the project. The average time per note (including recording of the bibliographic details) was 6.5 minutes (range: 3.1 to 11.6 minutes). When they finished their report, the students were asked to count the total number of notes taken and the total number of notes actually used during the writing of the report. The average number of notes taken was 52 (range: 17 to 204) and the average number of notes used was 38 (range: 32 to 73).

A significant fact flowing from this study is that on average 5.63 hours was spent just writing out the notes. That time does not include the reading and thinking time prior to notetaking. Given that on average only 38 of the 52 notes were actually used in the written assignment, about two hours of notetaking time proved to be immediately useless.

The lesson to be learned from this study is: be sparing in your notetaking. Ask yourself before taking a note: How is this information relevant to the topic and where can I use it in the essay? Those two questions will save you a lot of time—and a lot of head scratching (which many students do at the writing stage when they confront notes with little apparent relevance to the topic).

Notecards v. paper

For the first three years at university, I used tablet paper to take notes for essays, reports and other written assignments. As many students who use this medium discover, they end up with many bits of paper which are just plain awkward to handle and organise. A friend suggested notecards and there has been no turning back since then.

Notecards do cost a bit more than tablet paper, but their redeeming features are uniform size (get cards about 7.5 × 12.5cm), durability and manageability. They can be stacked, shuffled, dealt into piles and carried easily. For the convenience of typists, the cards can be alphabetised quickly by author's name to generate the reference list. Having described the benefits of notecards, you will want to know how the cards are to be used to make the system work well.

On one side of the card record in clear handwriting (especially if someone else will be typing from the cards) the bibliographic details. If more than one note is taken from the same source, simply put, for example: Meyer (1972). This denotes that the full bibliographic details are available on the first Meyer notecard. You will need a separate notecard for each individual note, in case you want to use any one note in several different parts of the assignment.

You will see from the illustrated notecard which I used when writing this book that the bibliographic details are clearly written on side A. The tick in the lower right corner signifies that the card was used in the text writing. The note in the top left corner of side B tells me where I thought the note might be used. The

SIDE A

Bibliographic information

Clanchy, J. & Ballard, B.

Essay Writing for students

Melbourne: Longman Cheshire, 1981

✓

SIDE B

Notes

Ch 6 - redrafting - or final checklist - adapt

checklist

( ) too long or too short?
( ) topic question answered?
( ) all important areas covered?
( ) logical development of ideas?
( ) all sections logically linked?
( ) satisfactory balance in treatment
       of topic?
( ) effective introduction & conclusion?
( ) phrasing precise and accurate?
( ) voice and style appropriate?

note about the checklist is a paraphrase of the original and as you can see from the top note, I was uncertain whether to use it in the redrafting section or as a final checklist. I opted for the latter as you will see at the end of this chapter.

In recording the bibliographic information on your notecards, be certain to adhere scrupulously to the reference convention of the school or discipline for which the essay is being written. Unfortunately, the convention for history differs from that used by most psychologists, so be certain you know exactly how your reference section should be structured.

When considering where your note may be used, you might think of several different parts; for example, including a brief mention in the introduction plus a citation in section A-2 of the body. By specifying where you can use the information, you will avoid wasted time and energy in taking superfluous notes and you will also expedite the writing of the first draft.

Specific mention must be given to paraphrasing, the process of boiling down the essence of the source into your own words. Many students avoid paraphrasing (the process can be difficult at times) and take far too many direct quotes from the source material. Your markers are not wanting to know how proficient you are at copying quotes from reference sources, but they are very interested in assessing your ability to critically analyse the thoughts and views of others. Thus, when considering taking a note, ask yourself: How does this relate to the overall topic? What is the basis for this view? Are there any assumptions which need to be clarified? The note should be *brief* and preferably in your own words.

In summary, notecards are a very manageable medium on which to record your research notes. Put the bibliographic notes on one side. On the other, record the section of the essay where you intend to use the note and then briefly record your paraphrased note plus any critical thoughts you have about the matter.

Sort your cards and refine outline

Having researched, read and noted issues and ideas relevant to the topic, it is now time to sort your notes to assess exactly what you have before commencing writing.

Start sorting your cards by allocating them to piles representing each of the sections of your preliminary outline. Thus, you would have a pile for the introduction and separate piles for each of the major concepts in the body; and a pile for the summary/conclusion.

Now read through the notes in each pile and look for a logical path which connects the issues. For example, are the concepts in the body based around a compare and contrast theme (differing views about some central idea) or perhaps they represent a developmental sequence (tracing the history or growth of a phenomenon). Finding a logical path which can link your ideas and research findings is often difficult, but absolutely crucial. Without this unifying stream, your essay is likely to end up as a muddy backwater with lots of ideas just floating loosely around.

If your research notes do not adhere closely to your initial outline, then you might have to restructure the outline. When radical restructuring is necessary, you might well have to return to the library for further reading and notetaking. The object is to develop a tight and concise treatment of the major theme of your essay. To dive into writing with irrelevant and tangential ideas will irritate your marker and produce a poor result. The returned essay is likely to be adorned with comments such as: irrelevant, ambiguous and waffle. So, be certain to have refined your outline and researched your ideas as thoroughly as you can prior to writing.

First draft—start writing!

The day has arrived when your schedule says, start writing. In spite of all the reasons which you will undoubtedly be able to offer as to why writing must be delayed, it is imperative that you start the first draft *today*! Most students will hastily explain: 'But I've still got so much reading to do. I've not covered all of the topic.' Those are very familiar words to my ears and to those of many teachers. The reason for the procrastination is that students feel inadequate in their knowledge of the topic.

Case study: Anna, the procrastinator

At this point, it might be helpful to present the case of Anna, a third year law student and a habitual procrastinator. Over her first two years of law studies, she consistently failed to submit her assignments on time. When given extensions by the more compliant staff, she still was unable to get her assignments in by the revised date. By third year the staff had had enough of her unreliability. They told her to submit her work by the prescribed date or fail! Anna responded with determination, but when the first submission date arrived, she became sick with various aches and pains. She obtained a doctor's certificate for a week's sick leave and finally submitted the assignment four days after returning. As there were medical circumstances involved, she did not fail, but she was penalised twenty per cent for the four day lateness.

Anna's doctor referred her for counselling when she developed a chronic spasm of her writing hand, a problem which made any writing very difficult. Also she was having stomach upsets, frequent headaches and chronic diarrhoea. Her doctor could find no medical reasons for these problems and deduced they were all related to her excessive and quite unrealistic fears that she was going to fail. I treated her with relaxation training plus a rigorous challenge to her pessimistic attitudes about her academic potential. Fortunately, the staff cooperated when Anna told them she was obtaining treatment for her procrastination problem. After several months of treatment, she was able to start her assignments very early and with the exception of one paper, she handed them in on time and received high marks for her work.

For those of you who share Anna's problem, discuss your situation with a counsellor or another helping professional who is familiar with fears of failure. The problem can be treated and the results are positive, if the procrastinator is willing to work very hard.

Apart from fears of failing, other students can experience mental blocks when attempting to write their first draft. They have done their reading and researching, but just can't get started on their writing. A functional suggestion is to sit down, take pen in hand or place your fingers on the keyboard and start writing or typing. The first several lines might be absolute nonsense, but that won't go on for long. Sooner or later, you will tire of seeing random letters being recorded and your mind will get into a more constructive mode. It might sound simplistic, but the task is to get moving on the topic and any movement is better than mental and physical paralysis which can drain your confidence and waste your time.

If this 'hand in motion' approach fails, try presenting your ideas to a friend or colleague, as suggested earlier. Be certain to find a new and uninitiated person to listen to your briefing; otherwise, you are likely to be seen as an academic bore by your selected circle of briefing partners.

Plagiarism

Plagiarism is an academic crime of representing the thoughts or ideas of someone else as your own. In most educational institutions, students who are found to have plagiarised are dealt with very severely.

In writing your first draft, it is imperative that you adhere scrupulously to the conventions for citing sources of the ideas which you use. If you have directly quoted someone in your draft, you must signify their ideas by quotation marks and identify the publication source and page number. For paraphrases, quotation marks are not used, but it is wise to acknowledge the source. Depending upon the discipline for which you are writing, the style of citing these references will differ. If you are in doubt, ask the teaching staff for the correct citation style.

Productive writing

Many part-time students are going to have difficulty finding sufficient creative time to sit down and write productively. The work day will generally offer few if any opportunities for creative thinking and assignment writing. The evenings of class lectures will probably be equally busy. That leaves several open evenings and the weekends for writing. There is simply no easy way to deal with this problem. The plight of the part-time student is a difficult one and survival means confronting the time squeeze and finding a coping strategy. Whether you write in short spurts or need a protracted period of peace and quiet, it will be up to you to find the time.

In order to discipline your writing, try to set daily goals. Try not to buy into the common argument which many students present: 'I need to get my adrenalin flowing before I can really write.' Unfortunately, this state of tension often appears only the night before submission day. At this time, tension can quickly escalate to full-blown panic which is not the best of emotional conditions for clear thinking and concise writing. The ideal goal, as stated earlier, is to get your first draft done about one week before submission date, giving you plenty of time to redraft and polish the assignment.

Redrafting

Most writers will agree that *good writing is good rewriting*. Your first draft will almost certainly read differently the following day. On the second reading, you will probably see logical inconsistencies or awkward phrasing which seemed to be acceptable previously. Spelling and grammatical errors might also appear. The redrafting process should cleanse these errors, omissions and oversights from the draft. Don't hesitate to shuffle the order of the paragraphs and to carry out other types of radical script surgery. It is far better that you do it then have your marker suggest it.

A mention about word processing must be made at this point. For those readers who are proficient at using a WP, as the equipment is popularly known, then skip over this section, for it will be preaching to the converted. All other readers should give very serious consideration to learning how to use WP software. Most large organisations and even many small businesses will have a WP on site and perhaps available to staff. Ask your employer about WP classes, as acquiring these skills might well benefit the organisation. The skills will most certainly benefit your future, as we become increasingly more computer based. The obvious academic reason for learning to use a WP is to draft and redraft your assignments. There is no more efficient way to do it. For the relatively small investment in time and energy, you can expedite your future assignments. Enquire about the possibilities of learning at work—another opportunity to obtain double value from your work experiences.

Use a checklist

While working on a large project, it is quite easy to overlook some details which might catch the eye of the marker. Use the following checklist prior to preparing your final draft to catch any deficiencies in your essay or report.

Sample checklist

Research
( )   Evidence of having found pertinent documents.
( )   Evidence of reasonably comprehensive reading.
Content
( )   Covered all parts of the question?
( )   Justified any conclusions reached?
( )   Opinions substantiated by adequate referencing?
Expression
( )   Spelling.
( )   Sentence construction.
( )   Paragraph structure.
( )   Transitions between paragraphs.
( )   Grammar.
Essay structure
( )   Introduction states essay topics, outlines scope, describes essay plan.
( )   Body covers all parts of essay topic and is free from irrelevant material and waffle.
( )   Conclusion summarises main points discussed in essay and restates the topic in the light of preceding discussion.
Technical detail
( )   Footnoting and text referencing correct?
( )   Bibliography complete and correct?

( ) Abstract included, if required?
( ) Correct length?
( ) Submission on time?
Presentation
( ) Title page.
( ) Margins.
( ) Legibility.
( ) Written on one side of paper only.
( ) Neat.
( ) Presented in folder, if required?
Final draft

Having ideally reworked your essay several times and hopefully slept between the redrafts, the time has come to prepare your final draft. If you have been working on a WP, then this stage presents very little additional effort. Following one final and critical reading with fine adjustment editing, just press the 'print' key on the keyboard and wait for the pages to roll out.

If, however, you have been handwriting or typing your paper, then considerable time will be necessary to produce the final copy. It is strongly advisable to get your final draft typed, as presentation does count. Imagine the case of the student whose handwriting is barely decipherable under normal conditions. The final draft is being copied by hand usually late at night after a long and protracted writing period—not the best of conditions for producing neat and legible work. If the paper were marked as the last in a stack of one hundred essays, you can imagine the reaction of the marker upon discovering that your handwriting is all but illegible. For handwritten essays and reports, be absolutely certain that your script is neat and easily legible. If friends consistently remark that your handwriting is impossible to read, then get your assignments typed.

Submit on time

Submission day has arrived. Having worked diligently on the assignment, you certainly want to get it to the marker on time. There are many tales of students who have entrusted a friend to deliver their paper, only to find that for various strange reasons the paper never reached the destination. Try to always deliver your assignments in person.

In large bureaucratic systems where you are not known by the teaching and clerical staff, it might be advisable to obtain a receipt if your paper is handed in at the faculty office. Prior to submitting your paper, be sure to take a copy so that you are covered in case the original is lost, mislaid or destroyed.

Learning from returned assignments

When essays and reports are returned, many students give a cursory glance at the mark and then disregard the paper. If the paper is placed in the lower drawer of your bedroom dresser, you are bypassing a most significant learning experience. It is hoped the paper has been marked conscientiously and the page margins will have copious notes about the strengths and weaknesses of your writing.

Even though rereading your paper might appear to be a boring task, the process can be a most significant learning experience. Take special note of the strong points noted by your marker (let's hope that your marker has recognised the educational benefits of rewarding good work!) and focus specifically upon the weak areas. If, perchance, your paper has very few comments to guide you in your future writing projects, then consult your marker. It is perfectly reasonable to ask for the paper to be reconsidered and for the strong and weak points to be identified. There is hardly likely to be a queue of people making this sort of request, so the marker should be willing to comply. If you are refused, then consider seeing the head of school. Teachers are paid to teach and giving substantial commentary about assigned written work is a clear expectation. You do not want to antagonise your marker unnecessarily, but if this clear duty is being ignored, then you have a justifiable grievance.

Checklist

( )   I start projects as soon as they are assigned by establishing a file and setting a weekly work schedule.

( ) I prepare an outline based upon a paragraph plan to guide my early thinking and research.

( ) When gathering information, I consider resources in addition to the libraries; eg, newspapers, questionnaires and personal interviews.

( ) Prior to taking a reference note, I question where I will use the information in the assignment.

( ) I use notecards to record reference information.

( ) I start writing my first draft *on time*, with plenty of time for rewriting.

( ) I polish the draft during several revisions prior to submitting the assignment on time.

Summary

Your assigned reports and essays will comprise a significant part of your final marks in most of your courses. Expressing yourself in writing is one of the most important skills to be developed during your formal education years. This chapter has presented a series of steps which can help to perfect your writing skills. The following topics were discussed in detail:

- Establish a project file.
- Set task and time goals for progressive stages of the project.
- Clarify the topic.
- Read for a preliminary understanding of the issues.
- Write a preliminary outline.
- Research the central issues.
- Take notes.
- Sort your notes into logical sets.
- Finalise outline.
- Start writing, on the scheduled date.
- Redraft and polish.
- Complete final draft.
- Submit on time.
- Scrutinise the returned work; learn from strengths and weaknesses.

7

Preparing for examinations

- *Timetabling for systematic revision*
- *Getting help early*
- *Learning how to relax*
- *Desensitising examination anxiety*
- *Performing well in essay exams*

The life of the part-time student is hectic enough. Examinations just contribute further chaos. The problems surrounding exams can be many and mixed, but perhaps you will recognise some of the following dilemmas.

Between work, home and personal responsibilities, there is simply no time left for examination revision. Your boss seems to place new and major work projects on your desk just prior to exam time. As you frantically page through your notes in the final week before the exams, you discover several points which you do not understand. All attempts to contact the relevant teaching staff prove futile. Because of work and study pressures, you lose several hours of sleep each night during the week prior to your exams. You are physically exhausted and emotionally fragile. The tensions surrounding your exams have placed your personal relationships at risk. Exams start and you still have one major assignment to complete! During the end-of-year rush, close friends ask: 'Are you OK?' You're looking off-colour.'

For many part-time students, these problems will be very familiar. You could probably add further issues which have fractured your studies and frustrated your progress. However, let's look at some central issues which should help to make your next examinations more successful. As this chapter will not deal with all issues involved in successful examination performance, the interested reader should consult the book, *How To Pass Exams* by F.E. Orr (Allen & Unwin) for a more full and detailed discussion of the salient topics.

Timetabling for systematic revision

One approach which will help most students to succeed in their examinations is to schedule regular weekly revision sessions. If you are going to try but one strategy described in this book, this is the one which is most likely to produce the greatest benefit in your final marks. What is involved? Simply put aside about two or three hours every week (probably best on the weekend) and do nothing during this time except revise for your examinations.

That sounds very simple and straightforward, doesn't it? But, most of you will quickly respond: There's no time for that! I know that your time is very limited and valuable, but focus upon your results sheet and suddenly your examination marks will be seen to be equally valuable. In fact, your examination marks will probably account for about 30–50% of your final marks; a very important factor to consider when allocating your time.

Phillip was just starting a plumbing apprenticeship and was working four days a week in a large manufacturing firm with one day in class at the local technical college. He had never really enjoyed school and his results from the past reflected his aversion to books and study. Now that he was employed and his job depended upon satisfactory progress in his studies, he was very keen to improve his performance. We mapped out a systematic program whereby he budgeted time for studying, and most importantly, for examination revision right from the start of his course. He was very pleased to receive his first academic report which showed all four subjects to be in the 80s. This positive reinforcement prompted a similar performance in the following two terms of the year.

Just as Phillip budgeted revision time right from the beginning of the year, it is most important for you to do the same. You might think that revising for final exams on the first Saturday or Sunday morning of the new academic year is absurd. Yes, that does seem to be a bit compulsive, but the earlier you start, the better will be the result. As mentioned earlier, you experience an 80 per cent memory loss of lecture material unless you revise your notes within 24 hours and regularly after that for a month or so. The more you routinely revise, the better you will be able to retain and reproduce the material in the examinations.

In your revision, go through the notes for each of your subjects and try to learn them as if you were going to be examined next week. As you progress week by week, link the previous work to your notes from the past week. Your weekly revision sessions will therefore result in a systematic learning experience.

Thus, examination success depends upon systematic and regular revision. Revise early in the academic year and continue every weekend. Discipline is required, but the results will make the effort worthwhile.

Getting help early

Many part-time students become frustrated in their attempts to obtain additional help from teaching staff. As most students attend evening classes, both students and staff are eager to dash for home as soon as their academic obligations are fulfilled. If, following a lecture, you are in doubt about the quality of your notes, speak to the lecturer straight away. If you delay sorting out the matter, subsequent lectures may well be confusing. Staff members can also be difficult to find later—especially the day or two before the next scheduled examination!

If you are not able to find a mutually convenient time to meet with a lecturer, then perhaps there are other resource people who can help. One pool of helpful people whom you should consult is your classmates. You can probably contact them on the telephone or meet on campus. A coffee meeting before, between or after classes can be both a pleasant social occasion and a helpful academic experience. Using your knowledge is one of the best ways of clarifying your understanding of lecture topics and enhancing your memory.

For major problems in your course work, you might want to consider finding a tutor. If your studies are aligned with the work you are doing, then there could well be a suitable resource person at work who might help you. Should no one be suitable at work, then consider seeing a private tutor. For common subjects such as English and Mathematics, you might find a suitable tutor listed in the classified ads of your local newspaper. Also check for listings of post-graduate students available for tutoring on your campus noticeboard. When help is necessary, be certain that you get it.

In summary, get help when you are not able to understand the classroom concepts. Waiting and hoping everything will clear up is courting possible failure. There are many sources of help including teaching staff, classmates, postgraduate students and private tutors. Be certain to obtain the help you need to progress in your course.

Learning how to relax

Probably the most common concern of students is fear of failure—or at least fear of not performing up to their desired level of achievement. Failing can be particularly traumatic for part-time students, especially those who are being partially subsidised by their employer. The signs of anxiety are extreme nervousness, pounding heart, rapid breathing, inappropriate sweating (as when sitting quietly and trying to prepare for examinations), weak concentration, queasy stomach, and a general state of agitation and restlessness. If any or (Heaven forbid!) all of these symptoms are common for you, then read on to learn how to deal with the problem of examination anxiety.

Belinda was an apprentice hairdresser who experienced extreme nervousness when performing various hairdressing skills on clients while her examiners watched. Her hands would shake and her voice would falter. She was also worried about her perspiration. Her anxiety was sufficiently obvious that one of her examiners suggested she obtain help. Following several months of treatment, she was able to perform in her final examinations with no obvious hand shaking. She felt much more confident about the technical hairdressing skills by knowing she could perform more calmly and competently.

Just as in the case of Belinda, the basic skill for most examination candidates to master is learning how to relax. By relaxation, I do not mean just physical relaxation, but more mental control. If you develop an effective power of mental control, then by quieting the mind, you can generally quiet the body. With examination anxiety, the body effects are usually the result of excessive worry about the result of the examinations. Of course, if you have done little or no work, then it is perfectly appropriate to worry about possible failure. However, there are students who work effectively and well during the term, but regularly fall to pieces in the examination room. These students can improve significantly by learning how to relax.

Mental control practice

- *Practise every day.*
  Learning how to relax sounds easy, but will take about two to three months of twice-daily practice to develop the skill. Two fifteen-minute sessions, one in the morning and one early evening are recommended. Do not argue that on busy days you are just too busy to relax. These are the days when you will need the practice the most.

- *Expect to relax.*
  Develop the positive expectation that you will relax. There is little benefit in yelling at yourself: *Relax! Dammit, relax!* as relaxation is a passive process. Just sit back and let it happen. Don't try too hard, but do try to practise at the same time every day, if possible.

- *Find a quiet place.*
  You can learn to relax almost anywhere. You really don't need special equipment or particularly quiet circumstances. Try to find a spot away from interruptions such as the telephone or workmates. Tell your workmates that you are learning how to relax and they will probably want to learn more about the technique themselves.

- *Make yourself comfortable.*
  Sit in a comfortable chair or stretch out in a quiet place. Loosen any tight clothing around your neck so that you can breathe comfortably. If you are worried about falling asleep (it can happen occasionally), then set an alarm for fifteen minutes to put your worry to rest.

- *Focus upon your breathing.*
  To start, close your eyes and focus your attention upon your breathing. Listen to the soft whistling sound which your breath makes entering and leaving your body. Breathe quietly and gently for about ten breaths, saying RE-L-A-X to yourself as you breathe out. Bar from your mind any problems, worries or concerns—think only about your breathing and say RE-L-A-X as you breathe out.

- *Relax your muscles.*
  By systematically relaxing the major muscles of your body,

you will be able to move into a deeper level of relaxation. Start with your forehead muscle. Think about this area and then say to yourself, *relax*. After a brief pause, think about your eyebrows and say, *relax*. Move systematically downwards through the body and relax the following parts: the cheeks, mouth, jaws, neck, shoulders, back, upper arms, lower arms, wrists and hands, chest, abdomen, thighs, calves, ankles and feet. For variety, you might want to try working upwards through the body during some practice sessions.

- *Focus your attention.*
  In order to further deepen your level of relaxation, fix your mind on a relaxing scene. Choose a setting which you have previously experienced as a quiet and relaxing place. In your mind, try to experience the sights, the sounds, the smells, any touch or temperature effects which characterise the place. For purposes of relaxation, it would be best to visualise a scene in which you are alone. For more detail, consult Chapter Seven of *How to Succeed At Work* by F. E. Orr (Allen & Unwin).

- *Use a positive self-suggestion.*
  Once you have developed a pleasant state of relaxation, then say to yourself a statement which will enhance your examination performance, such as: 'I can study effectively', or 'I can concentrate', or 'I will succeed in my course.' It is important to mention that using positive suggestions in the absence of any real and concentrated study effort is not going to produce a miraculous result. Perhaps the only result for these students will be a more comfortable failure. Regrettably, achieving high marks in most courses is going to require hard work.

- *Come back slowly.*
  In order to come out of your relaxation state, count slowly from one to five, allowing yourself to become more alert with each number. When you have reached five, open your eyes and then slowly stretch your arms and legs. Stay seated for a minute or two to allow your body to fully readjust to your normal state.

- *Plan your next relaxation practice session.*
  As mentioned at the beginning of this section, learning how to relax will require a lot of practice, perhaps two to three months of twice daily sessions. Plan your next session while you are enjoying the effects of your present relaxed state.

In summary, be certain to find the time to practise twice daily for about two to three months in order to gain the maximal benefit. Start your sessions with quiet and gentle breathing, followed by systematically relaxing the major muscles of the body. Then visualise a relaxing scene to deepen your relaxation. Use positive suggestions to enhance your relaxation practice or your academic performance. Gently return to your normal state and plan your next practice session.

Desensitising examination anxiety

Helen worked for the public service as a clerk and was the first person in her family to go to university. As her parents had no money to finance her education, Helen worked full-time and pursued her Arts degree part-time. Her father worked in a factory and boasted about his bright and very capable daughter who was the pride of the family. Helen felt pressured by her parents' high expectations and feared that she might disappoint them. The fears escalated at examination time each year when Helen fell to pieces and often was physically sick with vomiting, diarrhoea, shakes and shivers. Of course her examination performance suffered severely because of her sickness, which was diagnosed by her doctor as being psychologically based. She was referred to me for treatment of her examination anxiety.

We progressed through the relaxation training which was described in the previous section and then commenced work on actually reducing the fear of failure which she associated with any major assessment. The results were very positive, both academically and physically. Helen performed superbly on her examinations and survived the assessment period without any major illness, although she did have an occasional twinge of concern. Two years after treatment, she now enters the examination room with calm resolve and resilience and has almost completed her honours degree.

Just as in the case of Helen, you can rest assured that if you have studied conscientiously and know your work well, there is every chance that you will be able to perform more calmly and confidently if you work through the relaxation and desensitisation procedures. Remember to start early as the entire process can take several months.

Step-by-step anxiety desensitisation

Desensitising exam anxiety really means replacing your previous feelings of extreme nervousness with calmness, or at least firm mental control. This is done by first getting relaxed and then imagining examination-related scenes. The imagined scenes start with you preparing for your exams early in the academic year and progress to scenes of you in the examination room actually performing confidently and competently. The process is based upon a conditioning mechanism whereby you learn to pair a strong relaxation response with the word, *relax*. The trigger word, relax, is then used to produce the relaxation response while you are first imagining scenes and later when you are actually sitting for the examination.

In order to help make these scenes as realistic as possible, write out specific descriptions on separate cards, one scene per card. The ten or so cards are then sorted in order of anxiety potential, usually starting with a scene describing you studying early in the academic year (let us say, a low anxiety situation) and progressing to a scene of you actually taking the examination. Let's look at several sample cards.

Card 1

Day one of the course, and everyone is comparing timetables and talking about the subjects they are doing. Someone mentions how difficult the examinations are in this course. I am standing outside the room where my examinations will be held in four months. I can see the empty desks and the blackboard at the front of the room. There is an electric clock on the far wall which will time the examination.

Card 2

One month before the examinations. I'm sitting at my desk in my room looking at the list of outstanding assignments and thinking about my revision for the examinations. Four weeks to go and still so much to do!

Card 3

Two weeks to go and I am on a coffee break at work paging frantically through lecture notes. Every spare minute is being used to revise for the exams. A workmate asks how the preparation is going which prompts a surge of tension. I try to remain calm and confident about the coming exams.

Card 4

I am sitting in my last lecture before the start of the examination period. The lecturer is discussing the examination and the scope of the material to be covered. My mind continually darts back to previous disasters in examinations. I am fighting to remain calm during the class.

Card 5

The morning of my third exam and I'm walking up the stairs to the exam room. There is a lot of nervous chatter going on amongst the other students. My mind is racing through the topics which I think will appear on the exam. I approach the door of the examination room ...

The five samples above should give you the general idea of how to construct your own cards. Prepare about ten scenarios which progress from very low fear situations to the highest fear situation you anticipate experiencing. Arrange the cards in sequence from low to high and then number them, in case you drop the stack while deeply relaxed.

As systematic desensitisation is a very important and successful method for overcoming examination anxiety, it is worthwhile to summarise and elaborate on certain steps.

- Relax yourself thoroughly.

- When you are very relaxed, read the first card in the sequence. If the scene is set in your room, then while imagining, look around and see the various sights—the furnishings, pictures, posters, radio, etc. Note any colours, sounds, or even aromas. Make the scene as realistic as possible.

- Read each card and check yourself for any anxiety feelings or others signs of nervousness, such as pounding heart and increased breathing rate. If any of these signs are apparent, then say *Stop!* to yourself and picture a stop sign in your mind. The *Stop!* command will interrupt the scene which is causing the anxiety.

- Take a comfortably deep breath and say *relax* to yourself as you exhale to re-establish a relaxation response. Allow the tension and anxiety to flow out as you breathe out. Continue saying *relax* as you breathe out until you are thoroughly relaxed.

- Repeat the scene, experiencing the same details as you did previously. If you again experience feelings of nervousness and tension, repeat the *Stop!* command and then relax yourself.

- Keep repeating the scene until you can maintain it in your mind for fifteen to thirty seconds while being relaxed.

- When you have reached the point where you can imagine the scene for fifteen to thirty seconds while still being relaxed, advance to the next card and repeat the process.

- If one or more scenes prove to be particularly difficult, carry the relevant cards with you during the day. At coffee breaks or when waiting, consider the problem scene and feel yourself relaxing as you say *relax* to yourself.

- If you do not have days or even weeks to go through the entire desensitisation series, you can still derive some benefit by working through the scenes for a few minutes each hour. Yes, this is a last-ditch effort, but it's far better than going into the exams in a thoroughly frazzled state.

- If you can not conquer your anxiety and the situation is getting worse, consult a helping professional, doctor or psychologist for treatment. Obtain a certificate to document your difficulty and present it to the examination authorities.

Relaxing quickly in examinations

Many students may not have the time to learn the full techniques of relaxation and desensitisation before the start of their next series of exams. If this applies to you, then the following hints about how to relax in the exam room may be of value, both physically and academically.

- Be certain that you know the exact location, date and starting time of each of your exams so that you are not starting an exam in a nervous frenzy because of lateness.
- Periodically during the exam, close your eyes and take a comfortably deep breath and then let the air out slowly and quietly. Say *relax* to yourself as you breathe out.
- Dangle your arms by your sides to allow an easy flow of blood down to your hands and fingers. Gently make a fist in both hands and then relax, letting the tension flow from your finger tips.
- Change your body position slightly to allow more blood flow to your thighs, buttocks and back.
- Stretch your arms, legs and back.
- Take another slow and deep breath and say *relax* as you breathe out.
- Resume work on your examination feeling a bit more rested and relaxed.

In summary, dealing with examination anxiety will require an early start and an arduous campaign. Learn the art of mental relaxation and control of worries. When the relaxation response is well established, then apply the desensitisation procedure to neutralise any fears related to your examination performance.

Performing well in essay examinations

Writing essays under controlled examination conditions has

been a time-honoured tradition of student assessment in most academic institutions. Because the essay examination is so common, you are well advised to be listening during lectures for possible examinable topics and to be thinking about essay questions during your revision. Having prepared well during the academic term (this point can not be emphasised too much), you might well benefit from the following points.

- *Read and interpret the essay question very carefully.*
  You will get few, if any, marks if you misinterpret the question and produce an essay which has little relevance to the prescribed topic. In order to help focus your attention, re-read each essay question and then underline the key terms with a red pen.

- *Underline the key words.*
  The important words to note and underline are those describing the topic to be discussed and those specifying the operations to be carried out. You will want to be very clear about the latter. For example, the word criticise differs markedly from the word discuss. If you are not absolutely certain what the differences are between the commonly used operational terms in essay questions, then refer to pp. 106–7 in *How To Pass Exams* by F. E. Orr (Allen & Unwin).

- *Write down your initial ideas.*
  As soon as you have read the question, jot down your immediate ideas. At this stage, you want quantity of ideas—and hopefully there will be some high quality ideas amongst them.

- *Organise your ideas.*
  Now go through your notes and extract those which seem to be specifically related to the topic. With these key ideas in front of you, try to order them in some logical way. In order to win high marks, you will want to prove you know the key facts and concepts, but these ideas *must* be described in a logical way. If finding a logical structure for your essays has always been a problem for you, discuss the matter with a student counsellor experienced in examination problems.

- *Outline your essay.*
  Having found a logical pathway through your ideas, set them down in an outline on the first page of your examination booklet. Most markers are relieved to see some effort has been invested into organising the essay they are about to read.

- *Write the essay.*
  With an eye on the clock, start writing your essay. There are several points which might be helpful:
  —In the introduction, tell the reader how you have organised the essay.
  —Get right to the point; don't waffle.
  —Link your paragraphs with appropriate transitional phrases.
  —If possible, use the key terms in the question as you write your essay.
  —Summarise your major points at the end of the essay.

- *Check your essay.*
  Having completed your essay, read through it quickly before the end of the examination to check for misspellings and grammatical errors. These details can create a strong, negative impression upon the marker.

- *Scrutinise your marked essay when returned.*
  When you receive your marked essay, study it carefully to understand your strengths and more importantly to improve upon your weaknesses. If your essay does not have sufficient marker's comments to give you a full appreciation of your performance, then take your essay to your marker and request (tactfully) further clarification.

Brief mention must be made about hand writing legibility. If your family members and friends comment about the illegibility of your handwriting, there is every chance that your examination markers may also have difficulty reading your script. Practise writing for long periods, say two to three hours, and make a most deliberate effort to write very legibly. Have a discerning friend read the essay and give you some constructive comments about the quality of your writing—both ideas and script. You are likely to lose marks if the reader has to work very hard just to decipher what you have written, so practise and perfect your writing style.

Mastering other forms of examination

There are many forms of examination which are commonly used in educational establishments, including short answer, multiple choice, true–false, matching, open-book examinations, laboratory tests, and performance examinations such as the bedside medical *viva*. This book cannot do justice to all of these varied forms of examinations, but the interested reader should consult *How To Pass Exams* which was noted at the beginning of this chapter for further information.

Checklist

( ) I revise weekly throughout the academic year.
( ) I consult the teaching staff if I continue to have difficulty after trying to understand a concept.
( ) I do not allow confusion to accumulate.
( ) I relax daily to control any tensions, especially those associated with assessments.
( ) I can desensitise any particular anxieties which may affect me during examinations.
( ) I listen for good examination questions during lectures.
( ) I practise my essay writing techniques with some time pressure so that examinations are less difficult.
( ) I scrutinise returned exams to learn from my successes and errors.

Summary

Examinations account for a large percentage of the final marks for most students and this chapter has described various tactics which students can use to earn those marks. The following important issues have been discussed .

- Start early each year and systematically revise on a weekly basis.
- Get additional help as soon as you are aware that you do not understand the material being presented in class.
- Learn how to relax and then desensitise any fears about being assessed so that you can perform calmly and confidently in your next exams.
- Perfect your essay writing skills.

8
Keeping healthy and fit

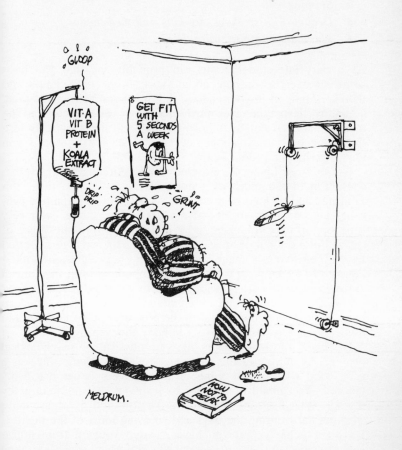

- ● *Eating a healthy diet*
- ● *Dietary guidelines*
- ● *Exercise regularly*
- ● *Sleeping well*
- ● *Dealing with smoking, drinking and medications*
- ● *Planning for your leisure time*

As a part-time student, you will probably say that you have sufficient exercise dashing about during your work hours and then sprinting off to your classes. Attaining and then maintaining a healthy lifestyle involves much more than just exercise and the ingredients need not be time-consuming and unpleasant. Before discussing how to go about getting and staying fit, see if you identify with the profile below.

I dash from home on most mornings skipping breakfast because I'm in too much of a hurry. By morning tea time, I'm famished and then gorge myself on biscuits to survive until lunchtime. I spend the majority of my work time sitting, with very little opportunity for exercise. When I have to climb a set of stairs, I'm often out of breath after just one or two flights. I often have a negative self image because I am overweight and unfit. I have given up smoking yet again and hope it will last this time. I crave an alcoholic drink at lunchtime to get me through the rest of the day. I am taking anti-anxiety, anti-depressant or sleep medication to help me cope with the pressures of work, study and home. I am too busy to have a holiday this year.

Do many of these factors fit your physical or psychological profile? As the life of the part-time student is frantic, there is a very good chance that some of these health issues are being ignored. You might quickly try to justify your health status by saying: 'Who has time for keeping healthy and fit when you're working hard during the days and studying most of the nights?'

It's quite likely that you have excused yourself from fitness programs because you are 'too busy'. However, while becoming healthy and fit does take time and effort, there are ways in which you can attain these goals and not jeopardise your work and study schedules.

This chapter will address several health and fitness issues

including diet, exercise, sleep, smoking, drinking, medications and leisure. These can be literally vital concerns, and the more hectic your life becomes, the more important it is to monitor and manage these health aspects.

Eating a healthy diet

One of the most routine experiences for many people is eating, which can be very pleasurable, but also problematic. Even though eating is a biologic necessity, the basics of good nutrition are often misunderstood and frequently abused. This section will discuss some general issues relating to foods and eating and will present some general guidelines for a healthy diet. A sample diet will be presented followed by a problem clinic.

Eating food is for most of us one of our first and also last pleasures in life. While eating is necessary for life, many people misunderstand the essential nature of food and the reactions these foods have upon their body. Ideally, food should be considered to have nutrition value only. Eating should not be used as a reward, nor food deprivation used as a punishment.

While nutrition and dietetics go beyond the scope of this book, it is important to alert readers to one of the most common eating problems—obesity. Many workers and students are overweight, simply because their daily schedule involves too much eating and too little exercising. Relatively few part-time students schedule regular exercise to balance their food intake, generally because they are too busy. Instead, many pursue magical diets which seldom offer any long term solution. The ultimate solution to obesity is self-understanding with a generous portion of discipline, a well-planned diet and regular exercise—not easy, but very effective. Let's look at a case study to see how diet and body weight can affect your work and study performance.

Daphne sought counselling because she was depressed, fatigued and lacked motivation in her job and studies. She was in her second year of an interior design course and felt she had the potential to be in the top 5 per cent of her class. However, her marks were falling precipitously and she was frightened of failing.

Part of her fatigue problem was attributable directly to her diet. She was 11kg overweight and was frequently trying new wonder diets. Following a short, but intensive period of deprivation, she would return to her snack-eating pattern. Predictably, Daphne reported she was too busy to get any regular exercise, but claimed that she frequently had to walk about the office or make outside visits to clients.

The following guidelines were part of the program recommended to Daphne and they could well help you to establish a healthy diet and lifestyle.

Dietary guidelines

- Focus upon getting fit and healthy rather than just losing weight.
- Plan for both exercising and healthy eating. Get professional advice about the most beneficial exercise possibilities for you.
- Enlist the support of others living or working with you. Changing your eating and exercising habits can at first cause some personal inconvenience and some mild discomfort. The battle will be fought more easily with good support and encouragement.
- Consult a nutritionist from your state health department for advice about good foods for you.
- Avoid snacks. If you must nibble, try celery or carrot sticks.
- Refrain from eating in front of the TV. Limit your eating to one place, generally the kitchen or dining room.
- Never eat when standing up—a good way to exclude eating snacks.
- Eat slowly and savour each mouthful. Swallow slowly and enjoy the pleasant sensations of eating and tasting.
- Be aware of boredom eating. Many people who have weight problems eat because they are bored. Investigate new hobbies and interests to keep busy and interested.
- Limit your sugar intake, both obvious (on cereal, in drinks) and hidden (in cakes, biscuits, etc).

- Substitute complex carbohydrates (grain products, fruits, vegetables) for refined sugar. The complex carbohydrates will supply energy for longer periods and they contain other nutrients as well.

- Don't keep sweets, chocolates, cakes, biscuits and other problem foods around the house or work place. Put temptation at a distance; the longer the distance, the better the resistance.

- If you miss the crunch of crispy snack foods, try banana chips, sunflower seeds, carrot or celery sticks and fresh apples.

- Decrease your salt consumption. It's a cardiovascular stressor.

- Monitor your alcohol consumption. A standard drink of beer (200 mls) or a glass of wine has 500 kilojoules and no other nutrients. Dilute wine with mineral water or alternate sips of wine with sips of water.

- Place a food consumption chart on the fridge door and record what you eat.

- Use small plates and don't keep the serving dishes on the table so that you can help yourself to additional servings.

- Don't shop when you are hungry. Restrict your food purchases to the items on your shopping list.

- Chart your daily weight each morning to monitor how your eating and exercising plan is progressing. Don't expect instant results from a new diet/exercise program. Be satisfied with a regular loss of about a half to one kilogram a week.

- Limit your caffeine intake to 500mg per day, the limit of your liver in detoxifying the caffeine. (One average strength cup of coffee contains 100mg of caffeine, and tea, about 65mg.) Try drinking herbal tea, refreshing and non-caffeinated beverages.

While these are general guidelines, you may wish more specific suggestions such as the sample diet below. If the suggestions do not agree with your food preferences, then consult a nutritionist for alternate ideas about a healthy diet.

A SAMPLE DIET FOR WORKER/STUDENTS

Breakfast—not to be missed
  Plain cereal, left over boiled rice or boiled wheat with just a sprinkle of sugar. If
    you choose other cereals, check the salt and sugar content on the package.
  Wholemeal toast or bread, but delete margarine, butter and jam.
  Fruit juice or a piece of fruit.
  Tea or coffee, preferably black.

Lunch
  Wholemeal bread sandwich with any protein-rich filling (eg, cheese, egg, cold
    meat).
  Salad with lots of green vegetables, no oil dressing.
  Piece of fresh fruit.
  Tea or coffee, preferably black.

Dinner
  Choose a lean meat from fish, veal, chicken or have a vegetarian main course.
  Whatever your main course, serve with appropriate vegetables (steamed) and
    potato, rice or pasta.
  Dessert, if necessary, can be rice pudding or a cheese platter.
  Tea or coffee.

While the diet suggests certain foods as being desirable, there are also some foods which should be monitored carefully and consumed sparingly: sugar, oil, butter and margarine; foods eaten in moderation include milk, cheese, yoghurt, lean meat, poultry, fish, legumes, nuts and eggs; and foods which should be eaten preferably include cereals, bread, vegetables and fruits.

It is important to reiterate that the diet outlined above is a general guideline. To make it work for you, it will be necessary to incorporate variety and some creativity to render the foods appealing and satisfying. Once again, consult an experienced nutritionist for further advice about modifying your diet to accommodate a healthier lifestyle.

The success of your diet ultimately comes down to personal discipline and the types of thoughts you have about yourself and your dieting goals. Dr Albert Stunkard, an American psychiatrist, has reported several common self-talk arguments which can undermine a diet:

Positive responses to problematic thinking and eating

● *'It's taking so long to lose weight.'*

'Yes! But I'm losing it and this time I'm going to learn how to keep it off!'

- *'I've never done it before. Why should I succeed this time?'*
  'There has always got to be a first time and this time I will make it!'

- *'I keep finding myself thinking about how good chocolate tastes.'*
  'Stop that sort of thinking! It's only frustrating you. Substitute a thought about you relaxing on a beach or having some other kind of pleasant experience.'

- *'Everyone in my family has a weight problem. It's in my genes.'*
  If that is the case, it just makes the task harder, but not impossible. I will lose weight if I use more energy than I take in.

These internal mental monologues can be critical to the success of any dieting program. Be certain to monitor what you are thinking about your eating and dieting. If you are uncertain about how your thoughts are affecting your eating behaviour, consult a psychologist and discuss the matter. Generally, how you behave is a product of what you think. If you can get control of your thinking, you have a much better chance of succeeding.

In summary, the worker/student's diet is very important. The foods eaten morning, noon and night can affect the quantity and quality of one's work and study as well as influence the way we feel about ourselves. Eating wisely can make you a more productive worker, a more effective student and overall a more happy person.

Exercise regularly

The important role of exercise was mentioned in the preceding section. Quite apart from contributing to correct weight maintenance, exercising on a regular basis can keep you physically fit and emotionally sound. But where do you start and how do you go about regaining and then maintaining a physically fit body?

Many people who trained regularly and seriously for competitive sport during their school years will recall the pain and agony experienced during the training sessions. Yes, rigorous training is exhausting but often exhilarating. But having prospered from these training experiences years ago, should you go back to the same regimen to get fit again? Decidedly not! The former athlete who tries to step briskly and vehemently into the old training program (even if it was only a year or two ago) risks injury to the muscles and bones, it not more serious medical consequences.

Four steps to a healthier body

The person who is unfit and decidedly plump may be embarrassed at even the thought of going to a gym where everyone appears to be fit and firm. Speak with an experienced fitness instructor about your feelings. There could be special 'getting started' classes nearby which cater to your special needs and sensitivities. The important point to keep prominently in mind is that you can become more healthy and fit, but you have to make a start. How should you get started on your fitness campaign?

Step 1   Start carefully and slowly

See your doctor and have yourself checked for participation in a fitness program. You might wish to consult a fitness specialist at a reputable gym or at a nearby university. Essentially, you want to find an exercise program which is: (1) enjoyable; (2) convenient; and (3) suited to you at your age and condition.

Step 2   Calculate your exercising heart rate

The essence of an exercise program is to use the large muscles of the body in a repetitive fashion such that you increase your pulse rate to 70–85 per cent of its maximum level. You can calculate your exercising heart rate by subtracting your age from 220, the average maximum heart rate, and multiplying this figure by 0.75. For example, a 20-year-old person would ideally exercise at or about the following rate: $220 - 20 = 200 \times .75 = 150$ beats per minute. In order to measure your heart rate, take your pulse for ten seconds below your thumb on your wrist or below the end of your jaw on the side of your neck. A healthy 20-year-old person should try to maintain a pulse rate of between 125–150 beats per minute over a 20–30 minute period for maximum effectiveness.

For sedentary workers who have not exercised for years, you are advised to work up to this level over a time period recommended by your doctor or exercise consultant.

Step 3 Choose an appropriate exercise

You may find that brisk walking, cycling, swimming, Tai Chi, yoga or dancing, may be appealing. They are all beneficial types of exercise. Jogging, for some people, is too jarring and traumatic —see your doctor if you are in doubt about the suitability of jogging for you. Other exercise options include skating, skipping rope, rowing, and exercising to music. In order for you to gain maximum benefit, it will be necessary to have some form of exercise about three to five times per week. Studies have shown that at this rate there were fewer injuries and accidents, possibly because the body has time to rest and repair between exercise sessions.

Step 4 Maintain the program

Part-time students entrenched in work and study pressures can quickly dismiss scheduled exercise. However, it is very important to recognise that your exercise sessions will enhance your work and study effectiveness and give you a necessary and beneficial break from 'the grind'. We can easily take our health for granted—until, of course, we incur ill health. One way of getting your exercise automatically is to cycle or walk to work. This option will not be possible for everyone, but those who live reasonably close to their work can commute and exercise at the same time. Other exercise suggestions include:

- Never take lifts or escalators when you can climb the stairs (unless your work location is on the 40th floor of a sky-scraper, in which case take the lift to floor 35 and walk up the remaining flights).

- Park your car several blocks away from your destination and walk the remaining distance. You might find better parking opportunities at longer distances from work or campus.

- Do some exercises frequently throughout your work day such as stretching your arms and legs, bending your upper body and twisting your torso.

- Do isometric exercises while sitting or standing at work. Simply press your hands down upon the desk top for about fifteen seconds at about three quarters maximum tension. You can carry out similar exercises for your leg and torso muscles, but obtain advice from an exercise specialist.

Having extolled the virtues of regular exercise, a few words of warning are necessary. Exercise can be taken to extremes and become harmful, even addictive. If you find that: you are ignoring your work and/or study responsibilities in order to exercise; or, you are reacting with crankiness and irritability when you miss a day of exercise; or, you are going out to exercise in extreme weather conditions which could be potentially dangerous, then perhaps you are exercising too much. Use good common sense so that your body will benefit from your exercise program.

In summary, exercising regularly each week is important to your physical health and your work and study performance. See your doctor before starting fitness training and consult an exercise specialist about a suitable program. If discipline is not your strong suit, then pair up with a friend and get fit together. You are much more likely to make that extra effort to get to your exercise venue if your friend is waiting for you to arrive.

Sleeping well

Following on from diet and exercise, a third fitness factor which is important to the part-time student is sleep. As basic as sleep is there is still a gap in our scientific understanding about what actually happens during this resting stage.

While the reason for sleep remains obscure, we do know that there are two types of sleep—rapid eye movement (REM) sleep and non-rapid eye movement (NREM) sleep. REM sleep is lighter than sleep during the NREM periods. As for dreams, they occur during the REM periods and it is perfectly possible to have several dreams in one night.

Many people worry about the amount of sleep they are getting or missing. Some think they are sleeping too much and others worry they are not sleeping enough. The vital question which most ask is: 'How much sleep do I need?' The answer depends upon the individual. Some people are comfortable and work well during the day with as little as three or four hours' sleep at night. Others may feel they require as much as ten or twelve for effective daytime functioning. Current sleep researchers have found that the average sleep period reported by research subjects is seven and three quarter hours.

Sleep experts suggest that a person has a sleep problem only if the inability to sleep interferes with daytime functioning, no matter how many hours are spent asleep. Thus, if you sleep for only a few hours most nights, but still function well most days, then a sleep problem does not exist. There may be, however, a bed problem or a sleep partner problem which warrants attention.

Sleep problem

In order to establish whether you have a sleep problem, it is helpful to look closely at the following questions:

- When am I being troubled by the sleep problem? Getting to sleep? Waking frequently during sleep? Waking early and not being able to get back to sleep? Or, feeling sleepy during the day?

- Have I had this sleep problem for months or years, or is it a recent problem? If the problem is a recent one and there are obvious causes such as pain, worry, anxiety, or other problem states, then the sleep problem is of less concern. Healthy individuals who generally have been sleeping well in the recent past can tolerate quite substantial sleep losses in the short term and still function reasonably well. However, depending upon the individual and the circumstances, there is a limit to how much sleep and rest deprivation can be tolerated. See a doctor if the sleep problem persists.

- Can I do something about the cause of my sleep problem, if the cause can be identified? Possibly yes. For example, what can be done about the traffic noise outside the house to which you have just moved? Problem sleepers should have looked for a quieter street, but given the existing conditions, can you erect a front wall or plant several noise deflecting trees? What about installing a lattice screen outside the bedroom window and grow climbing plants up it? Can heavy and lined curtains help? Ask an architect or consult a noise expert at a local building information centre. There are often practical approaches which can be applied to sleep problems. Just trying to do something about the problem will at least resolve some of the frustration. One of the most common sleep problems is insomnia.

Insomnia is the inability to fall asleep or to stay asleep for a sufficient period of rest. There are three variations to this sleep problem: tossing and turning at bedtime and not being able to get to sleep; waking during or through the night, interrupting the sleep process; and waking too early and not being able to get back to sleep.

Insomnia can have many causes and it is best to discuss the problem with your doctor. In many cases, insomnia can be related to a physical illness, to pain in your body, or to any one of several different psychological states including depression, anxiety, or intense worry.

Another cause of insomnia is excessive arousal before going to bed. While regular physical exercise is generally beneficial, it can cause body arousal and hence interfere with the onset of sleep. Various foods can create problems also, such as caffeinated beverages (coffee, tea and chocolate) and spicy or gaseous foods. It is best to avoid these foods if you have a problem with sleep.

Sleep can be interrupted by breathing difficulties (annoea) or by snoring. Both of these problems can be caused by mechanical obstruction of the airways. A common factor associated with these obstructive problems is obesity. People who are overweight and carrying excess tissue in the neck area can experience breathing difficulty from these tissues constricting their upper airways. Research has shown that a 10 per cent loss in body weight can solve or at least improve the sleep problems attributable to airway constriction. In addition to losing weight, here are some other suggestions for improving your sleep.

Better sleep suggestions

- Towards the end of the day, taper off slowly so that your mind and body adjust to a slower pace. Expecting an instantaneous change from high activity to sleepfulness can be expecting too much.

- Practise the relaxation technique described in the previous chapter. Focusing your mind upon the relaxation technique will preclude worries and other arousing thoughts from disturbing you. Sleep will come when your mind is quiet and relaxed.
- Exercise regularly, but not just before bedtime.
- Try soaking in a warm bath to relax yourself.
- A glass of warm milk is a time-respected sleep enhancer. It's worth a try.
- Avoid caffeinated drinks just before bedtime.
- Reading can help if the material is not arousing.
- Avoid sleep medication as drug dependence can occur.
- If the sleep problem persists, see your doctor.

Smoking, drinking and medications

These three health issues are major concerns and a definitive discussion goes well beyond the scope of this book. However, it is important to deal at least briefly with each issue.

The health consequences of tobacco smoking are well publicised and documented. The evidence is conclusive that tobacco smoking is related to a wide variety of health problems, including lung cancer, cardiovascular disease, pulmonary problems, to mention but a few. While it is each individual's right to decide whether or not to smoke, it is not fair to affect those in the immediate vicinity. Increasingly, non-smoking zones are being established in more public places and many offices and educational institutions are restricting smoking to areas which are not going to affect non-smokers. If you work in an area where smoking is presently permitted and you are concerned or annoyed by tobacco smoke, discuss the problem with your boss. If you are a smoker and want to give up the habit, consult your state health department, the cancer council or your doctor or other practitioner for advice.

Alcoholism and problem drinking are also major worries, both at work and at home. Drinking on the job is not generally condoned and, if discovered, often warrants a stern reprimand from management. However, reprimands can be ineffectual when there is a well-entrenched drinking problem. If you depend upon alcohol to get you started at the beginning of the day and are sneaking drinks during the day, you probably have a serious drinking problem which should be addressed. The first step towards recovery is admitting that there is a problem. Your family doctor or Alcoholics Anonymous are good sources of assistance.

Just as alcohol dependency can undermine your work and study effectiveness, there are other dependency-inducing drugs which can cause similar problems. Some of the most commonly abused drugs are the minor tranquillisers (Valium and similar medications), headache pills, and sleeping tablets. If you have been taking any medications for a long period, see your doctor to have your situation re-assessed. Some adjustment in the dosage level of prescribed drugs may be possible or there could be alternatives to medication which can be explored.

Plan your leisure activities

Most readers will be familiar with the adage: All work and no play makes Jack/Jill a dull person. Many major business firms are now taking that saying to heart by encouraging their employees to become involved in hobbies and other interest activities. These firms know that many workers accumulate tensions and worries on the job. By having some regular avocation or interest, these people can release the tensions and thus be happier while on the job.

'But what can a hobby do about a real work problem?' you might justifiably ask. The hobby itself is not going to solve a problem, but it can provide a positive distraction so that the worry is not going to concern you continually. A hobby or interest could well extend you academically, socially or psychologically.

Almost any type of hobby will do. The essential quality should be your basic interest in the activity and a desire to work at it. However, it is important that you don't transfer a work problem to a hobby activity. For example, Ian was a very dynamic and aggressive 28-year-old stockbroker and part-time Master of Business Administration student who was at his office at 7.15am every weekday (and some weekend mornings as well). He faced a continual onslaught of problems and decisions at work which caused a major stress problem. His doctor suggested that he pursue a hobby and so he returned to tennis, a game he had played at school. However, his tennis games were characterised by the same ruthless, almost savage competetiveness that was creating his stress problem at the office. If stress is a problem, then look for leisure activities which are at the opposite end of the stress scale.

One final word about leisure and work—do not defer taking your holidays. Getting away from work and studies can make you a happier person and a better and more productive worker and student. When you are away, resist the temptation to study. Plan a variety of non-academic activities for your holidays so that you can return to work and study truly refreshed.

Checklist

( ) I eat a well-rounded diet daily.
( ) I resist snacks between meals.
( ) I keep any problem foods at a distance.
( ) I consume alcoholic beverages in moderation, if at all.
( ) I try to avoid sugar and salty and fatty foods.
( ) I talk rationally to myself if/when I have to modify any problem behaviours related to eating.
( ) I exercise appropriately three to five times per week.
( ) I sleep well.
( ) I do not smoke.
( ) I rarely take any non-prescribed medications.
( ) I take my yearly holidays and enjoy the break from work and study.

Summary

This chapter has presented several approaches to a healthier, happier and more productive work and study life. Being healthy will make you a more satisfied and productive person. The following issues were discussed:

- Maintain a nutritionally sound diet.
- Participate in a regular exercise program.
- Sleep well.
- Decrease smoking, drinking and non-essential medications.
- Pursue hobbies and interests outside the work place.
- Take your holidays regularly to recharge your batteries.

9
The plight of
mature age students

- *Special problems*
- *Common fears*
- *Dealing with problematic relationships*
- *Boosting your confidence*
- *Partner jealousy*

You're considering joining the swelling ranks of mature age students and probably feeling a little shaky at the prospect. You have been thinking about the possibility for some time and perhaps a friend suggested you take a more active step. Or maybe you have seen ads in the papers for mature age entry programs at various tertiary institutions. Whatever the source of your interest, you are probably thinking about some of the following issues.

- Will I be able to cope with the difficulty of the work?
- How will I get along with all those younger students?
- Writing essays frightens me. I have difficulty coping with letter writing to friends.
- I haven't done any mathematics in years. Learning the new maths may be beyond me.
- My partner may not like my going back to study. I won't be much fun with my nose continually poked in a book.
- Can I manage the studies in addition to my job? My boss may not be too pleased.

For workers contemplating studying part-time or even full-time these issues are probably very familiar. Mature age studying does pose special difficulties: coping depends upon determination; succeeding requires true grit. Let's look at some of the special problems confronting mature age students.

Special problems

Brian was 47 when he decided to leave his very successful position as a national sales manager and pursue an Arts degree with a major in psychology. He finished his secondary education at 1 and soon afterwards entered the sales field. While he was weak in mathematics, he was particularly skilled verbally and thus was able to mask his educational deficiencies.

However, when he started psychology he had to face statistics, a topic which both mystified and frightened him. Rather than turn tail and quit, he sought extra help from tutors. With hard work and perseverance, he succeeded. Not only did he complete his psychology degree, but he went on to finish a masters degree as well. Brian's years as a university student were essentially enjoyable, but there were some very bumpy periods of personal uncertainty, financial stringency and marital disharmony. He survived personally and financially, but his marriage did not. Brian though, is happier within himself for having completed the degrees.

Brian's case brings out several issues which often affect the mature age student: personal uncertainty, marital problems and financial stresses. More will be said about these issues later, but let's look now at another case study which presents some other common mature age student problems.

Yvonne was a single mother of three young school-age children. She had left her university studies when she married at 19 and soon afterwards had her first child. Her marriage broke up after the birth of her third child five years later and Yvonne struggled ahead, living on a pension and doing some casual work whenever possible. The office work never really challenged Yvonne and she craved more demanding responsibilities. When she mentioned to her mother her plans to return to study, the idea was met with scepticism and scorn. Her mother immediately questioned her motives and expressed concern about Yvonne's children. In spite of this negative reception, Yvonne pressed ahead.

Her major interest was hotel management and she had finally saved enough to pay for two of the three years of the course. However, early in her second year, the funds were running short and Yvonne had to drop from full-time to part-time study. While studying part-time, she started a small typing/secretarial business. The business thrived and Yvonne hired another single mother who was also a part-time student. Their business partnership and their studies were both very successful, mostly because they managed their time well.

Yvonne's case highlights several additional problems of mature age part-time students: scepticism from family and friends, child care concerns and time management problems. Having looked briefly at several mature age part-time students, let's now turn to the issues which might make studying easier for you.

Common fears

Mature age studying (the exact definition of mature age depends upon the institution) can be a frightening prospect in many different ways. Older students often question their academic potential and their personal stamina. Financial worries are very common as are fears about employability when they finish their course ('Won't I be too old to get a job?'). Let's look at each of these concerns separately.

Academic potential

As time goes by since one's last year in formal education, it is very common to lose personal confidence in learning. Most mature age students experience a classic conflict: I think I can succeed, but I don't like the possibility of failing (or at least not performing to my expected standard). Specific concerns mentioned by many students are their self-perceived inability to concentrate, remember, write essays and to handle mathematics.

'I'm too old and my brain's too withered to study well and compete satisfactorily with all those younger students' is a common sentiment. Many seem to think that their brain is no longer capable of handling a study routine.

Some pessimistic students might argue that we normally lose brain cells by the thousands every year once we pass the mid twenties. Despite this perfectly normal loss of neurons, our abilities do not decay precipitously. Even at the advanced age of 75 years and above, some people are still able to study very effectively. As the adage says: Where there is the will, there is a way.

Returning to the age range, 20–50 years, of most mature age students, let's look at the common experiences of fear and anxiety. Generally, these feelings thrive upon uncertainty. If you do not know the actual facts and details about what is involved in mature age study, then you are vulnerable to anxiety. In the absence of facts, uncertainty is often associated with thinking about problems. Take the following positive steps to prevent these negativities.

Positive approaches to mature age study:

- Talk with an admissions adviser where you intend to study and obtain information about mature age student 'survival' rates. You will probably find that mature age students fare very well in academia.

- Meet with some mature age students to discuss how they have managed their studies, work, homelife and relationships.

- Participate in orientation programs which will acquaint you with study and library skills, the administrative operations of the institution and other important student information.

- Get to know your teaching staff. See them as colleagues in a learning venture and not solely as judges.

- Be certain you understand specifically how you will be assessed in each of your subjects.

- Share resources with other students to lighten your load.

- Socialise with other students between classes. Learn from them and realise that even the brightest have both strengths and weaknesses.

Can I succeed?

Personal fears about returning to study revolve fundamentally around the question: Can I succeed? No one can supply the answer to this question but you. If you have progressed to the point of obtaining information about mature age study and you have not been turned off the idea, then the next step is to try. First-hand experience is the only way to ultimately test your potential.

The very fact that you are mature in age means that you have a relatively wide range of experiences to guide your future path and decisions. Many mature age students discount their personal experiences and life skills saying that they aren't relevant to studying. However, three of the most basic qualities for successful study are determination, discipline and diligence.

In order to boost your confidence and allay your fears, examine your past accomplishments, no matter in what area. For example, raising children or working successfully in a job both require ample quantities of the 3Ds. Write down your strong points, but with fairness in mind, note your weaknesses as well. While being fair, don't be modest. You want to objectively appraise your potential for this new venture.

Having listed your qualities on paper, have the sheet appraised by a close friend to ensure that you have not overlooked other important qualities. Once your self-appraisal has been validated as being correct, develop the strong attitude that I *can* do it. Get up each morning and repeat this positive statement to yourself. Spend some time each day planning and implementing steps which will take you closer to success. A step each day will deliver you to your destination.

Financial fears

Financial fears often put intending students off their target. However, financial problems can be solved if you are willing to make some adjustments. Before taking on a course of study, you might well profit by speaking to a financial consultant. Your local bank manager will be able to help assess your financial position, but prepare a comprehensive listing of personal expenditure before the meeting. Include all of your recurring costs and any anticipated major expenses during the period of study. Take into account how much time you will have available for part-time work. As mentioned in the preceding chapter, you need some relaxation time in order to keep mentally and emotionally healthy. Be careful not to overly commit yourself and thus wear yourself down.

Professional fears

'Will I be able to get a suitable job after I finish my studies?' is a frequently asked question. The employment market varies considerably across vocational fields and opportunities do change with time. Despite these fluctuating variables, you can get some idea of your future employment potential by speaking with a government employment officer who should have forecasting figures available.

You will also certainly profit by speaking with several people who are presently working in your major area of vocational interest. When speaking with them, ask the following questions: What are the major satisfactions in your work? What are the dissatisfactions? How did you train for your work in this area? What would you do differently if you were to start again?

After speaking with several people working in your proposed area, you should have some idea about your suitability for, and opportunities in, that job area. It would certainly be worthwhile to keep in touch with these people over the forthcoming years to monitor any changes in the employment market. Also, these contacts might well be handy when you are looking for a job.

Thus, fears which relate to your academic, personal, financial or professional situation are best confronted directly. Obtain specific information to ascertain the exact picture in each of these areas so that you are not hounded by fears based upon factual uncertainties. Once you have the facts, direct your attention at the problem points. Do something constructive about the problems rather than worry and fret. Solutions exist to most problems, if the problem is clearly understood.

Dealing with problematic friendships

Interestingly, major sources of concern for many mature age students are the derisive comments and the unspoken but loudly visible attitudes of their 'friends'. Many of these so-called friends may be jealous of your study plans. They too may have had some inclination to go back to study, but deferred because of the fears noted above. Others may see your plans to study as a move up the socio-economic ladder and away from them. Instead of welcoming this move, they slyly deride and condemn your plans and progress.

How do you deal with this difficult problem? Frankly, by developing a thick skin and by strengthening your belief in yourself and your motives. You really cannot control what others say about you, but you are in full control of how you feel about yourself. This is the area where you can make changes.

Boost your confidence

To deal with the negativities which may be directed your way, either verbally or visually, try the following confidence boosters to get you through these difficult experiences.

- Mentally cancel any lingering worries about back-biting comments with the *stop* sign technique. Picture a stop sign whenever you begin worrying what others are thinking or saying about you.
- Replace negative thoughts with a firm, 'I *can* do it!'
- Find friends who see your positive qualities and who make you laugh. Nurture their friendship.
- When facing large and challenging academic tasks, break them down into small and more easily managed jobs.
- Plan at least one positive event each day and look forward to it.
- Make a list of things at which you are good. If modesty interferes, ask a close and trusted friend to compose a list for you.
- Remind yourself that daily practice will help you to improve.
- If you intend to study in a professional or trade course, make a simulated business card with your name and academic credentials (to be acquired). Place the card in front of your desk to boost your determination and drive.
- When faced with unrelenting sniping or back-stabbing, confront the person pleasantly and ask if you can help them with their problem.
- Celebrate Wednesday afternoons. (Why not?) Half the work week is gone and only two days to go until the weekend. Share this celebration with a good friend as the sum of two people enjoying a good time is far greater than the arithmetic total of their individual pleasures.

● If the pressures and problems do get you down, arrange to have a talk with a counsellor. Just talking about your situation can make you feel better.

Practical pointers

As suggested in the case studies noted earlier in this chapter, managing your time is particularly important if you are pursuing part-time studies as a mature age student. While your situation is probably quite different to those of Brian and Yvonne, the time constraints remain the same—you have just 24 hours per day to use to your best advantage. Here are some practical pointers which might help.

● Use a TO DO plan every day to organise your tasks.
● Record your own revision notes on audio cassettes and play them while commuting, walking, waiting or while doing housework.
● Delegate as many domestic tasks as you can to free some time for study.
● Get to know other mature age students so you can share resources.
● Practise saying No! to yourself and others to remain in control of your time.
● Challenge any persistent worries which take valuable time. Solve any practical problems during a problem solving period each evening.
● If self doubts plague your study time, say to yourself, I *can* do it! and then turn your concentration back onto your studies.
● Talk with other mature age students and exchange ideas on how they manage their time; you can learn valuable lessons from others who have experienced the same time problems.

As a general principle, look for opportunities in your daily life when you can do two things at the same time. Revision can be done while commuting, washing the dishes, ironing and cooking. Ask yourself while you are performing manual tasks whether you might also be exercising your mind. You will develop your own time-saving strategies with a time-sensitised mind and a motivated mission—to succeed in your studies. For more specific suggestions about time management strategies, read Chapter Two in *How To Succeed At Work* by F. E. Orr.

Partner jealousy

Many mature age students confront criticism and negativism from their partner when their study plans are announced.

When the female partner in a relationship expresses interest in studying, there are certain reactions from the male partner which can cause concern. Some men react with jealousy, fearing that his partner is going to leave him behind intellectually. The jealousy might even be socially or sexually based with the husband suspecting that his wife is going off to meet other men to have an affair.

Apart from jealousy, some marital partners fear that their previous free time will now be taken up with their partner studying, precluding any leisure time together. If the partner is not supportive to the point of helping with the shopping, cooking, cleaning, managing and financing, then time for studying becomes very limited indeed. There is no really easy solution to entrenched and severe jealousy. Sensitive communication and delicate negotiation may help, but jealousy is often rooted in the self confidence of the jealous partner and not necessarily connected to external events like study. If the problem cannot be solved with several discussions, suggest that you meet with an experienced counsellor to help you both work through the issue.

The situation is often quite different when the male partner studies part-time. Generally, the studies relate to his work and the female partner may see the time spent studying as a step towards better career prospects. The combination of long hours at work followed by evening classes and then many hours in isolated study contribute to the phantom partner syndrome. In order to maintain a satisfactory relationship under such circumstances, both partners must make a strong effort at communicating and relating in their few hours together each week.

It is reassuring to know that despite difficult conditions posed by part-time study, studies have shown that very few marriages dissolve because of study factors alone. Readers can refer to the research on mature age students by Hore and West and summarised in their book, *Back To School* (Methuen, 1982).

Checklist

( ) I have appraised my potential for mature age study as realistically as possible.

( ) I have discussed the situation with family, work colleagues, and any others with whom I am closely associated.

( ) I believe that success is generally the product of personal determination, daily diligence and discipline.

( ) I have discussed any financial concerns with an appropriate consultant, eg, bank manager.

( ) I have a vocational plan and have discussed my goals with key people in the field.

( ) I feel comfortable about consulting teaching, counselling and other staff about any difficulties which might occur.

Summary

Part-time studying as a mature age student is difficult but certainly not impossible. The mature age student brings to the classroom and study desk life experiences which often help to make the task easier than initially expected. This chapter has presented a range of issues which address the plight of the mature age student, including how to:

- Address positively any personal doubts about your academic potential.
- Approach your studies with determination, discipline and diligence.
- Confront any fears about personal, financial or professional suitability by replacing doubts with data. Research the issues and clarify uncertainties.
- Deal tactfully but firmly with any sniping or back-stabbing 'friends'.
- Boost your confidence when your motivation wanes or withers.
- Manage your time.
- Deal with a jealous partner.

10
Rigours of
correspondence study

- *Types of correspondence study*
- *Special problems*
- *Coping strategies*
- *Practical pointers*

Simon left school early after completing year eleven to help his family financially. However, seven years later, he needed the extra education to progress at work. During the intervening years, he moved through several different jobs, but then found his vocational niche—technical sales. Having worked as a sales representative with a high-technology agricultural equipment company, he wanted to move into sales management and marketing. In addition to providing advancement, higher salary and more challenge, the management position would also mean less travel, a feature which would appease his wife and three children who were complaining about his long field trips. Simon's district manager told him that a mangerial position would be contingent upon gaining further educational qualifications, preferably a diploma or possibly a degree.

Because of his frequent absences from home, evening study was not feasible. The only other recourse was correspondence study. He enrolled at his local technical college to complete his higher school certificate over a two-year period. The course required firm time management and a very disciplined approach to his studies. His wife did complain occasionally about his long periods of isolation when he was studying, but she knew his course would give them greater freedom in the future. Recognising his career potential, his employer encouraged Simon by sponsoring him for a summer program in managerial skills.

Simon completed his higher school certificate in minimum time and enrolled in a part-time diploma in business management with a major in marketing. His career flourished as he progressed academically. The studying was indeed a hard grind, but the end result more than justified the effort. He is presently the state sales and marketing manager of his firm. Based upon his own experience, he encourages younger staff who have not completed their formal educational qualifications to consider correspondence study.

As Simon discovered, correspondence study is definitely not an easy option, but it is often the only recourse. This chapter will discuss some central issues in studying by correspondence including the following topics: types of correspondence study; problems in studying by correspondence; coping strategies; and new technologies.

Types of correspondence study

Correspondence study is basically education via the postal system. The educational institution mails lessons to students who then complete and return them for correction and marking. Most correspondence schools send out copious course notes and reference materials which substitute for classroom presentations. The student reads through the notes, perhaps several times, and then completes and submits one or more written assignments. These assignments are marked and a comment sheet is completed by the teacher. The marked assignments and comment sheets are mailed to the student who ideally studies them and then progresses to the next assignment.

With the advent of electronics and the popular usage of radio, audio cassettes, television, video and most recently, computers, the scope of correspondence study has broadened considerably. Students can now listen to radio broadcasts of lectures or listen to audio cassette recordings mailed to them by the sponsoring institution. Lessons which might be difficult to present in writing or by audio cassette, might now be presented on video cassette. This is particularly true for practical courses which have laboratory experiments or other exercises which can be supplemented beneficially by a video presentation.

Increasingly, correspondence students can 'speak with' their teacher and other students using computers with electronic mail facilities. Of course, all of these technological advances can only be used if the students have the appropriate equipment. But, quite apart from equipment and technical matters, there are personal issues which have presented problems for many correspondence students.

Special problems

As suggested in Simon's case, there are considerable difficulties to confront in correspondence study. Essentially, the types of difficulties can be divided into personal and technical. Let's look first at the personal difficulties, including low motivation; poor self-discipline; faulty organisational and goal-setting skills; and ineffective reading techniques.

Personal difficulties

To be successful at correspondence study, firstly you will have to develop strong powers of self-motivation. Studying by corres- pondence is lonely and isolating and most students report that they miss the classroom interaction with classmates and staff. When studying by mail, the individual must somehow generate the motivation and excitement which are generally part of the normal classroom experience.

When the correspondence student is sitting alone at home and there are no classes to attend, then studying can become a second order priority. The reading can generally be put off until a more suitable day when 'I'm more in the mood'. It doesn't take very many of these low motivation days to put the student behind schedule. The further behind the student gets, the more difficult it becomes to prompt the study effort. With dwindling confidence and tardy assignments, the student becomes disenchanted with the program and many fade from the rolls of the correspondence program.

The above scenario of low motivation is true for about 40 per cent of correspondence students—the ones who do not make it. Statistics show that the younger students are more likely to drop out, primarily because studying on one's own is such a lonely and alienating experience.

Insufficient personal discipline plagues all kinds of students, including those studying by correspondence. When daily living is filled with work, domestic duties and personal responsibilities, it is very difficult to fit in some studying. This is particularly true when there is no face-to-face contact with teaching staff to prompt a more diligent study effort.

Procrastination—a very easy pitfall for the correspondence student. Successful correspondence study depends upon a steady work output. Tomorrow is not good enough; why not today?

Organising sufficient study time is another problem area. The student must learn early in the correspondence course to practise planning. No matter whether the student has an abundance of time or very little, planning is very important.

In addition to these organisational and planning concerns, the student must be able to set specific goals. The staff of most correspondence schools will usually advise students how to go about setting out their study schedule, but the task of getting to the assignment and sticking with it is the responsibility of the student.

One additional personal skill area which is important for successful correspondence study is reading. As most correspondence work is done through the written medium, poor readers are going to be at a decided disadvantage. Reading is addressed in chapter four and the correspondence student is advised to read this chapter and then apply its principles. With regular practice, your reading efficiency will improve markedly.

Technical problems

Aside from the personal problems encountered by most correspondence students, there are several technical problems worthy of comment. The first is postal delays. Having mentioned this problem, there is unfortunately not very much the student can do to rectify the matter. Regrettably, we are at the mercy of the bureaucracy. If you experience repeated poor mail service, then write to your local post office manager and send a copy to your member of parliament. It is hoped that these letters will get through and the matter investigated.

Mail delays are not the only pitfall for the correspondence student. Recently, I made a videotape for a continuing education program and copies were sent to the enrolled students. The mail service in this particular instance functioned well, but a student's videotape machine did not. The playback system failed and the tape was ruined.

Other mishaps can occur with computer equipment. I should

warn correspondence students who are communicating with their instructor by computer-modem linkups, that power surges in the local circuit can create havoc with computer functioning. While using my computer at home to write a previous book, I became aware of a power variation problem. My wife put a load of wash in the washing machine and when it started, my screen blipped momentarily, indicating a problem. When I tried to save the last several pages of text, there was nothing there to transfer onto the disk. The power surge had wiped the information from the computer's memory. I now monitor the washing machine very carefully. If you use a computer at home and you do not have a buffer to block power surges, then have a bell placed near or on top of any applicance which draws considerable current. Better yet, remember to save your material *frequently*.

Coping strategies

Roger had been working as a clerk in a local government office. As with Simon who was mentioned earlier in this chapter, Roger had left high school early and worked in several jobs before starting with his present council position. He was aware that his letter and report-writing skills needed considerable improvement and enrolled in a correspondence course for remedial writing skills. He hoped that by improving his writing skills, he would be promoted to a more responsible position. On top of his work obligations, Roger also played for a local football team and trained two evenings a week. There was little time left for working on his writing skills, but Roger was determined to get his promotion.

He realised that once he arrived at work, there was little, if any, time to progress with his correspondence assignments which required a lot of thought and care. He decided to get up at 5am three mornings a week and work for two and a half hours on his assignments. Much to his surprise, he worked extremely well during these early morning sessions, primarily because there were no outside interruptions and he was able to concentrate all of his energy upon his work. In addition to progressing well with his course, he found that waking early got him off to a very positive start in his job. The course did take sightly longer to complete than initially anticipated, but the end result was that Roger earned a course certificate plus a promotion six months later.

Not all correspondence students can expect such positive results. As mentioned earlier, 40 per cent of enrolled correspondence students do not follow through and complete their courses. The problems of disciplined study and effective time management account for many lapses, but the motivation factor is crucial for most. Of course, having a promotion hinging on your course results is a significant motivator. However, for those students not in the workforce, you will have to generate your own motivation. This section will look at several practical and helpful pointers to boost your motivation, as well as some suggestions for improving your performance generally in correspondence study.

Practical pointers

- If your correspondence course is related to a job promotion, remind yourself about the benefits of the new job whenever you need a motivation lift.
- Make a business card for yourself with your name and the qualification you are working towards. Look at the card whenever you need a motivational boost.
- Cancel negative thinking by picturing a stop sign and staying *stop*! vehemently to yourself.
- Practise positive self-talk, saying I *can* do it! to boost your performance. These affirmations will create a state of positive feeling that is much more likely to prompt constructive action.
- We are never de-motivated. It's just that our motivation has been misdirected when we experience lapses in productivity. Dig down within yourself and search for your motivational energy and re-direct it into more constructive tasks.
- We often realise our dominant thoughts. Work conscientiously at making motivated and productive thoughts the dominant ones in your mind.
- Speak with people who have succeeded in a similar field to

the one in which you are involved. Ask them how they were able to achieve their goals and then learn from their experience.

- Find a friend at work or in the community who might enjoy studying by correspondence as well. Meet regularly to discuss mutual progress.
- Look for opportunities to accept more responsibility at work, at home, or in your community (to a reasonable level). You will have heard the expression: When you want a job done, give it to a busy person. Get busy and you will probably find that you become more efficient.
- Apply for a promotion. If rejected, ask what you have to do to be eligible for one. Suggest the possibility of enhancing your qualifications.
- Work to a daily plan, but occasionally focus your eyes on the far horizon so that you have long term goals to work towards.

Thus, motivational factors are generally central to the success of most correspondence students. Work actively at thinking positively to keep your studying as productive as possible. Look for the motivational energy that is within you and keep it activated. Use external reinforcers such as possible promotions or other self-development factors.

Time management and organising skills

While motivational factors are very important, you will also need to be in very tight control of your time. Time management strategies were discussed in chapter one, but a few additional ideas might be helpful for the correspondence student.

- As with the case of Roger noted earlier in this chapter, try getting up early and do your studying before your normal work day begins.
- Chart the number of hours of successful study so that the graph becomes a positive visual reinforcer.
- Set specific and realistic study goals. Reward yourself for fulfilling these goals.

- Keep a clock nearby so that your mind is time-oriented.
- Be prepared to say No! to anyone (including yourself) who attempts to distract or disturb you while studying.
- Keep a log of any major worrying thoughts which interrupt your concentration. Devote some time to solving the real problems, but dismiss any unrealistic matters which are silly and eroding of your study time.

Checklist

( ) I have a clear understanding of my reasons for studying by correspondence.

( ) I take every opportunity to communicate with the teaching staff, including telephone calls and participation in residential seminars when offered.

( ) I work to daily and weekly goals to get my assignments done and submitted on time.

( ) I am interested in learning about computer applications to correspondence study.

( ) When the pressure is on, I am prepared to rise early to get my studying done.

( ) I try to link my studies to my work goals.

( ) I keep my boss informed about my progress and discuss possible promotions when appropriate.

( ) I think positively about my potential for success.

( ) I manage my time carefully for my studies.

Summary

Correspondence study is particularly demanding. Providing the motivation and discipline is your responsibility. This chapter has discussed various types of correspondence study and some common problems experienced by these students.

- Study by mail, by computer or by audio and video-tape.
- Be prepared to motivate yourself.
- **Manage your time well to ensure that your assignments are submitted on time.**

- Be prepared to study in isolation.
- Be prepared to persist—achieving a diploma or degree will take years of study.
- Follow the practical pointers discussed earlier to maintain momentum and maximise motivation.

References and suggested reading

Clanchy, J. & Ballard, B. *Essay Writing for Students* Melbourne: Longman Cheshire, 1981

DeBono, E. *Lateral Thinking* New York: Harper & Row, 1973

Ellis, A. & Harper, R. *A New Guide to Rational Living* N. Hollywood, CA: Wilshire Book Co., 1977

Fensterheim, H. & Baer, J. *Don't Say Yes When You Want To Say No* New York: Dell, 1975

Greenberg, H. *Coping With Job Stress* Englewoodcliffs, NJ: Prentice-Hall, 1980

Hore, T. & West, L. *Back To School: a guide for adults returning to study* Sydney: Methuen, 1982

Lakein, A. *How To Get Control of Your Time and Your Life* New York: Peter A. Wyden, Inc., 1973

Marshall, L. & Rowland, F. *A Guide To Learning Independently* Melbourne: Longman Cheshire, 1984

Orr, F.E. *How To Pass Exams* Sydney: Allen & Unwin, 1984

Orr, F.E. *How To Succeed At Work: gaining the psychological edge* Sydney: Allen & Unwin, 1987

Index